Common Sense Storage

Clever Solutions for an Organized Life

Creative Publishing
international

MINNEAPOLIS, MINNESOTA
www.creativepub.com

Creative Publishing international

Copyright © 2010
Creative Publishing international, Inc.
400 First Avenue North, Suite 300
Minneapolis, Minnesota 55401
1-800-328-0590
www.creativepub.com

Printed in China

10 9 8 7 6 5 4 3 2 1

President/CEO: Ken Fund

Home Improvement Group

Publisher: Bryan Trandem
Managing Editor: Tracy Stanley
Senior Editor: Mark Johanson

Creative Director: Michele Lanci-Altomare
Art Direction/Design: Brad Springer, Jon Simpson, James Kegley

Lead Photographer: Joel Schnell
Set Builder: James Parmeter
Production Managers: Laura Hokkanen, Linda Halls
Page Layout Artist: Lois Stanfield
Edition Editor: Betsy Matheson Symanietz
Proofreader: Geoffrey Stone

Library of Congress Cataloging-in-Publication Data

Common sense storage : clever solutions for an organized life
/ created by the editors of Creative Publishing international.
    p. cm.
  Summary: "Inspirational photos and concise, practical
information on how to achieve an organized home"--
Provided by publisher.
  ISBN-13: 978-1-58923-568-7 (soft cover)
  ISBN-10: 1-58923-568-1 (soft cover)
  1. Storage in the home. I. Creative Publishing
International. II.
Title.

  TX309.C66 2010
  648'.8--dc22

2010025214

Contents

Introduction

Like most of us, you've got a lot of stuff. Maybe you've already tried to organize some of it into piles on the floor. Or maybe you've managed to cram much of it into closets, cabinets, and drawers that you're now a little nervous to open. You can't find things. You try to put things "away," only to find that there really is no "away" place to put them.

Relax—it happens to all of us. Without the right storage plan, the best we can do is fight a losing battle against the rising tide of clutter in our homes. Fortunately, *Common Sense Storage* can help you to reverse that tide, or at least to better steward it.

Whatever the scope of your ambition—whether you're looking to completely remodel or simply maximize the storage capacity of the existing space available in your home—you will find information and ideas in this book that will inspire you to find simple solutions for better organization in every room of your home.

In *Common Sense Storage* you will find hundreds of clear color photographs that showcase creative ways people have solved the same storage challenges you face. Enjoy reviewing them and we hope that you may learn from their experience.

Getting Organized

An organized home is a dream for many of us, and it's not because we long to win a home economics award. We know intuitively that the clutter in our homes reflects the chaos we feel in our lives. We live in a hectic world with dizzying schedules. A cluttered home, rather than providing the calm sanctuary we desire, compounds the madness and becomes just another chore to maintain.

Put simply, if you can't put your stuff away, you can't get away from your stuff. The clutter that overruns the physical space of your home will spill into your mental space as well. It is exhausting to spend your days putting random clusters of things into piles or constantly trying to find someplace to hide the clutter.

It doesn't have to be this way. Escaping this cycle isn't a pipe dream. It's a matter of shifting your focus from putting out fires to having an overall plan. It's all about organization.

Types of Storage

As you develop your home storage strategy, you'll need to determine where to actually store everything.

Active Storage includes those items you need access to all the time, such as clothing, food, and dishes.

Temporary Storage includes those things you don't need at your fingertips now, but will in the near future, like out-of-season sporting equipment. If you're not sure how often you'll need access to an item, it may be in transition to Inactive Storage.

Inactive Storage includes those things you either don't need anytime in the foreseeable future but want to keep (family heirlooms, memorabilia, children's clothing and toys that you may need again), as well as those items that you're not sure you need at all. Consider those items in a purgatory and possibly in transition to the recycling bin, charity program, or trash.

Active storage is a life saver in an entryway or mudroom. Take stock of your habits: What things do you bring in with you? And where do you throw them? Clutter gathers in high-traffic areas. If you take care of this often-neglected area, clutter won't migrate to the rest of your home.

Inactive storage should be housed in out-of-the-way spaces like attics, basements, or storage facilities.

Temporary storage should be readily accessible without occupying well-used spaces in the house. The garage is a perfect place for temporary storage.

The Decluttering Process

What do you have?

You can't design storage solutions until you know what it is you need to store. And to do that, you need to take inventory.

The hardest part is just getting started. So make it easy. Start by putting like things with like things.

This is a relatively painless process, and it doesn't involve any decision-making. Just put on some music and start creating piles, stacks, or clusters of things that belong together. If you have kids, get them involved. Make it fun.

If, as you sort, you discover things that obviously should be tossed or recycled, go ahead. But now is not the time to sift through papers, magazines, and collections to try to eliminate items. Just make the piles.

Then take a break.

Make sure you take a "Before Picture" so that you can see the progress that you've made. You'll be glad you did.

The "After" is worth it! The best storage solutions hide in plain sight, as is the case in this tidy guest room that utilizes hidden storage under the bed, in the headboard, and in the tucked away closet area.

What do you use?

Sorting your things into active, temporary, and inactive storage ultimately boils down to answering three simple questions: What do you need? How soon do you need it? How accessible does it need to be?

The easiest way to approach this problem is not to tackle every single item in your house, but rather to continue to work with the piles of similar items already clustered together. At this point, just try to place the piles in the rooms where they are most likely to be needed. Anything you think may be temporary or inactive storage you should place in separate remote storage areas.

It is unrealistic to think that you can make sense of it all in one frenzied afternoon or even a single weekend. Pace yourself. Start with small, manageable blocks of time, maybe 15 minutes a day. Once you get over the emotional hurdle and get some momentum behind you, try putting in two to four hours once or twice a week.

Remember to save your
receipts when donating to
charities. If you've done a
good job of de-cluttering
your home, odds are that
you've earned a healthy tax
break, too.

What can you live without?

There's a difference between "neat" and "organized." The house that is "neat" will have clean sightlines, but the drawers, cabinets, and closets may be repositories for randomly accumulated stuff. However, the house that is "organized" will be as purposeful with these hidden spaces as with what is out in the open.

In feng shui practice, any clutter in our homes will correspond with clutter in our heads. In terms of clutter, out of sight is definitely not out of mind.

So don't take your carefully sorted piles and stuff them into the nearest closet corner. Now it is time to purge yourself of what is unnecessary in your life. You'll feel better when you do.

If you just can't bear to get rid of something but think that it should be moved to inactive storage, keep it in a remote storage area for one year. If you haven't used it after an entire season cycle, let it go.

Having a place for everything discourages you from bringing unnecessary "stuff" home.

I give something up,
I get something in return.
—Thomas Moore

Now that you've uncovered what you have and removed the things you don't need, you're ready to find clever storage spaces for what's left. The rest of the book will help you do just that.

Insider Advice: Tricks from the Pros

Monica Friel, Professional Organizer, NAPO
Chaos to Order, Chicago, IL

Home storage is all about home organization.

- Set aside a designated time to work on a specific organization project. Working with a friend or a professional organizer can help you to avoid distractions.
- When you're motivated, dig into the hardest part of the project: the "weeding out." Be careful not to take on more than you can handle or you may end up with a greater mess than when you began.
- Don't create more chaos by buying storage bins before you've completed the weeding-out process. Oftentimes we buy more storage containers than we need and they end up causing the clutter they were meant to clear.
- When trying to determine if something is worth saving, ask yourself, "Would I take this with me if I were planning to move?" If so, it's worth keeping; if not, it's time to toss it.
- Before taking on a paper-organizing project, talk to your accountant to determine how long you need to save tax and financial records.
- Schedule for a pick-up of donations before starting the project, and use the pick-up date as a deadline. Knowing your old things are being passed on to a friend or a charitable organization will make it easier to let go of them.
- Remember, being organized is not about being perfect, it's about being efficient and having the time to do what's important to you.

Making a Plan

After the clutter has been cleared, in addition to having less stuff to deal with, you're also more familiar with how much stuff you have yet to find a home for. This is a great time to brainstorm on the function of each room to make sure your stuff—and the work you do with it—is in the right place.

For example, let's say your formal dining room has become the default location for bill-paying and general household paperwork. If this function has prevented you from using the room for special meals, the current setup is less than ideal. What you need is a dedicated office space.

A little thoughtful planning will lead you to the right solution. Perhaps you can carve some space out of a corner of the kitchen or living room—or remodel a closet into a hideaway office space. Taking a step back and thinking about organization and function throughout your home is the key to making sure you make the most of your home's space.

One way to plan new storage into your existing home layout is to print out a photo of the room or storage problem. Then, sketch ideas onto an overlay of vellum or tracing paper.

The best storage solutions fit with your everyday life. If your kids' favorite place to play is the family room, that's probably where the toy bin should go.

The Keys to an Organized Home

- **Efficiency follows reality.** Storage solutions must conform to the way you really live. If you tend to leave coats draped over kitchen chairs instead of hanging them in the coat closet, you need a better storage solution—perhaps a few coat hooks or a coat tree next to the entry door.
- **Store the most-used stuff close at hand.** Everyday cooking utensils and pots and pans should be reachable from the stove. Magazines and newspapers belong near your reading chair.
- **Beware of container clutter.** Too many boxes, bins, and bags can lead to more clutter than the stuff

itself. Weeding out excess items periodically and moving seldom-used things to long-term storage reduces the need for more storage vessels.
- **Keep it simple.** Complicated storage systems are bound to be ignored, especially by kids.
- **Leave room to grow.** Plan some extra room for the ebb and flow of accumulated stuff. Space flexibility helps contain clutter between periodic weed-out sessions.
- **Never trust your memory.** Clearly label all boxes used for long-term storage, or use clear plastic bins that reveal the contents at a glance.

Kitchens & Pantries

As the hub of the modern home, the kitchen presents some unique storage challenges; the biggest, perhaps, is providing storage for a vast and complex assortment of food-related items, from frying pans and corkscrews to linens and dishware.

Making sure that the things you frequently use to cook and prepare meals are accessible quickly is key to a smoothly operating kitchen. Combining open, display storage with more traditional closed storage, such as cabinets and pantries, often presents the best solution to this challenge.

The rooms on the following pages each utilize this strategy in a unique way, resulting in kitchens that are both visually stunning and fully functional social and creative spaces.

Cabinets

Store the utensils you use the most frequently in the open, near the range or other cooking surface.

Backlighting in the display case dramatically increases interest in what would otherwise be a room dominated by white.

This homeowner used semi-custom cabinets that closely match details in the nearby living room. On the short wall, vertical cabinetry maximizes the space available. On the longer wall, the cabinet doors are turned on their sides to mimic the drawers of the lower cabinets.

The horizontal doors also echo the look of the base cabinets, where deep drawers perfect for storing pots and pans are conveniently placed on either side of the stovetop. To accommodate the horizontal doors, the upper units are actually two 15-inch-high uppers stacked above a spice drawer component. Similarly, the raised portion of the center island is comprised of four horizontal upper cabinets with glazed glass doors.

Two completely different custom cabinet styles feel right at home together in this kitchen. The warm tones in the wood cabinetry below the counter space bring out the rich colors of the slate floor tiles. Above, the dishware behind the translucent doors is visible but not on display—that honor is reserved for the stainless steel countertop.

To create extra storage space out of ordinarily unused space, these homeowners built upper cabinets above and around the appliances.

Words to Know

There are essentially four types of cabinets:

- Stock cabinets come in a handful of sizes, usually in 3" increments, and can be purchased right off the shelves of many home centers. They are already assembled and ready to be installed, but are often unfinished.
- Components of ready-to-assemble (RTA) cabinets are available through home centers and furnishings retailers in a variety of standard sizes, door styles, and finishes. Each component comes in a flat box with easy-to-follow directions and guidelines for selecting related components.
- Like RTA cabinets, semi-custom cabinetry also comes in a variety of standard sizes, door styles, and finishes, but there are many more options to choose from. Unlike RTA cabinets, they are built-to-order and may be installed by the manufacturer.
- Custom cabinets are built by a custom manufacturer or cabinet shop. There are no standard components, so there are nearly limitless possibilities of sizes, styles, finishes, details, and accessories to suit your every whim. Besides offering the highest-quality materials and workmanship, custom cabinetry also eliminates the seams between components that are visible with the other cabinet types, and you will never have to use spacers to make a row of cabinets fit the available space.

Each option can vary markedly in quality, price, and durability, so if you're buying new cabinetry, it is important to learn as much as you can about the options before making a decision.

Sometimes even our best efforts to weed out the unnecessary in our lives still leaves us with too many things that need to be stored. That can be especially true in the kitchen.

The bare essentials for a functional kitchen can fit in a single unit sold at home furnishing outlets, which takes up less than nine square feet of floor space. So no matter what kind of kitchen you have, it probably has ample storage and workspace for one person. But for those of us who have growing families, want to entertain guests, like to bake, or just tend to buy groceries in bulk, we need as much storage space as we can reasonably squeeze into a room.

Handy bookshelves keep cookbooks within easy reach.

Adding a simple shelf transforms this wall into useful storage space.

This island is put to good use as an entertainment center on this side. It also creates a visual barrier separating the living room from the kitchen.

A kitchen island is a convenient prep surface for the cook, but it can also double as a spacious storage alcove on all sides.

Don't be afraid to use the space between the countertop and cabinets. Here, the few inches of vertical space against the wall create an artful glassware display that is easily accessible and aesthetically pleasing.

The built-in wine rack makes an attractive display and is convenient when entertaining guests.

"Enclosed" doesn't have to mean "claustrophobic." This beautiful built-in buffet effectively partitions the kitchen from the sitting room without isolating either space.

A generously sized center island and packed cabinetry around every appliance accommodates immense storage needs. A freestanding hutch in the open room not only helps reroute foot traffic to the dining nook, it also provides a few extra storage drawers and a tambour door for an extra appliance caddy.

The space above the microwave is perfect for storing cookbooks or Pyrex dishes used in the microwave, while the cabinet above is reserved for infrequently used items.

Insider Advice: Tricks from the Pros

Diana Allard, Organizing Professional, NAPO
Efficient Spaces, Plymouth, MN

Before setting items into any cupboard, line the shelves with light-colored shelf liner. Gone are the days of permanently affixed contact paper—today's versions come in various textures and designs and can be secured in place with or without tacks. Spongier liners cushion fragile items; smoother liners allow easy sliding. Using a light color in contrast to your cabinets ensures you'll see the items hidden in the back, darkened corners.

Organize pantry items according to use—placing all cans of soup or other quick meals in one area, baking ingredients in another. To maximize space, group items according to the type of container, such as cans, jars, or boxes. Finally, keep an item's double behind it, so it's clear when you've run out.

When buying spices, use a permanent marker or label to indicate the month and year of purchase. Most spices last a maximum of six to twelve months. Arrange spices alphabetically and/or according to use, such as savory versus sweet.

Keep toddlers in sight and out of harm's way with a kitchen "play drawer" filled with old plastic containers and other no-longer-used kitchen items. As children grow, give them the responsibility of setting the table with non-fragile dishes from this easy-to-reach drawer.

Add an elegant hutch to your dining area if you absolutely haven't any more room in the kitchen for cabinets.

If you need more preparation or storage space in your kitchen, consider adding a kitchen island or peninsula. An island can transform an otherwise unwieldy kitchen into a workable and efficient space for food preparation, eating, and socializing.

According to the Jenn-Air Homelife Trends Survey, the kitchen today rivals the living room as the primary place for people to gather and have conversations with family and friends. A center island can serve as a kind of roundtable that brings people together, offering a spiritual center for the home.

This classic, sturdy standalone island is the visual focal point of the kitchen. It provides a second sink, additional preparation surface, and extra storage on both sides. The butcher-block countertop is ideal for food preparation. Note that it doesn't match the rest of the counters: having a different countertop on the island can work if, as in this example, it harmonizes with other elements in the room.

Can't decide between a center island and an eating nook? Why not have both? In this kitchen, the island creates extra work surface as well as drawer storage for oversized items. The annexed table is not only a clever way to create an eating area, but it creates an inviting locale for people to congregate—centralizing the kitchen as a sociable, functional space.

It doesn't take long for that drawer you just organized to turn into the junk drawer filled with miscellaneous stuff that's hard to dig through. The deeper the drawer, the scarier the mess. Reclaim that drawer space and turn it from wilderness into accessible, neatly arranged space with these ingenious options.

This deep drawer with its sturdy center partitions provides enough space to store four neat piles of root vegetables, with easy access to ensure that you won't find new potatoes sprouting when you stock up for winter.

Glide out shelves make getting to the back of base cabinets much easier.

The movable and removable vertical rods in this drawer keep these stockpots neatly in place no matter how quickly and frantically the drawer is opened.

This slim pull-out bottle rack provides a tidy answer to the problem of storing liquid goods. You can always see the bottle in the back and you won't accidentally knock over other bottles to reach it.

This drawer makes effective use of space that would otherwise be difficult to access and organize with its four recycling bins. The containers for plastic, glass, metal, and paper are easily removable and kept neatly out of sight.

Every cubic inch of space is a miracle.

—Walt Whitman

It's not hard to identify the difficult-to-use spaces in your room, whether those spaces are hidden in dark corners—and those hard-to-use spaces are often in corners—or in plain sight. Maximizing your space not only gives you more room to work, but also helps you work more efficiently. Unclaimed space, ranging from a few inches to a few feet, can always be put to good use—for display, storage, or both.

This kitchen utilizes every available space for cabinetry, from floor to ceiling all around the room. Notice the narrow cabinets in the kitchen island and in the room's corners; fitted with dividers, these cabinets are perfect for baking sheets, cutting boards, and other flat kitchen accoutrements.

This is the classic alternative storage solution for that tricky corner space. The rotating shelf space of the lazy Susan lets you reach the items stored deep in the back with one simple spin. This lazy Susan features aluminum construction for a cool and contemporary look.

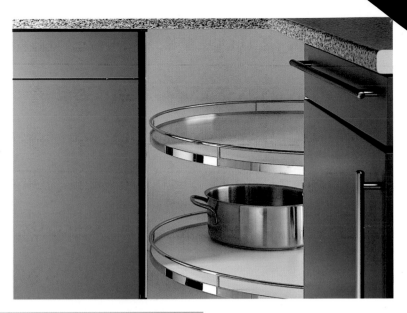

The glass shelving at the windows not only makes great use of the limited space in this compact kitchen, it creates a dramatic display as sunlight plays off the glass and ceramic dishes.

...in kitchens can be striking. Where above-counter cabinets
...e small kitchens, open shelving can create a lighter, more
...ironment, as well as easy access to dishes. In larger kitchens,
...ed shelf, dish rack, or pot-and-pan rack can create an
...g focal point to help break up the walls of solid cabinetry.

Pots and saucepans present a persistent storage problem, but here they are right at hand, just over the stove, neatly organized by size and color.

This rustic-looking kitchen appears so simple. Indeed, sometimes the simplest ideas are the best ones.

The objects lit on this wraparound display shelving draw attention to the dramatic wood beam construction of this kitchen.

The magnetic rack keeps knives accessible while freeing valuable counter space.

The open shelving keeps decorative glasses and dishware in view, while the topmost shelf extends out over the entrance to maintain a sense of continuity. The oversized island and the nook above the refrigerator provide additional display storage.

Insider Advice: Tricks from the Pros

Audra Leonard, Professional Organizer, NAPO
Artistic Organizing, Anoka, MN

- Every home needs a "landing pad," a table or counter near the entry where you can hang your keys, drop your bag, charge your phone, and sort your mail. Having a designated space for these daily items will keep them from ending up all over the house. Use a combination of trays, baskets, and bowls to contain the different items.
- When installing shelves, consider going all the way up to the ceiling. It creates additional storage and draws your attention upward, giving the illusion of added height.
- When displaying collectibles, put them in groups of like items or like colors. They will have more of an impact together and look less cluttered than if they are spread out around the room.
- Consider purchasing furniture that offers additional storage, such as end tables with drawers or ottomans that open up to reveal storage inside—perfect for blankets.
- Placing baskets or decorative boxes on open shelves gives you instant "drawers." Use them in any room to store everything from music CDs to bathroom supplies.

Sometimes cabinets are not the best choice to store your wares. It may be more convenient to have your things out in the open, or there simply may not be any room for more cabinetry. Your best friends in this situation are hooks.

Dishes are suspended above the sink to dry so that your dish rack doesn't clutter your countertop or sink.

Spices are kept right in front of the food preparation area without getting in the way.

Modular wall mounting systems are a wonderful way to free up your cabinet space while keeping the most-used items visible and within easy reach. Unlike cabinets, many of these systems can be expanded or altered as your needs change.

Build a Hanging Pot Rack

Why spend $150 to $300 to buy a hanging pot rack when you can build your own for under $20? Cut a pair of 1 × 3 stretchers at 36", then drill 1" holes every 8" on center. Cut 1" wooden dowels at 18", then glue and fasten them in place with 4d finish nails. Sand the assembled rack smooth and apply a water-based polyurethane finish. To hang the rack, thread four screw eyes into the top rails, connect zinc-plated chain to the screw eyes, and secure to the ceiling with heavy-duty J-hooks installed at ceiling joists or blocking. To hang your pots and pans, use appropriate-sized, zinc-plated S-hooks, available at hardware stores and home centers.

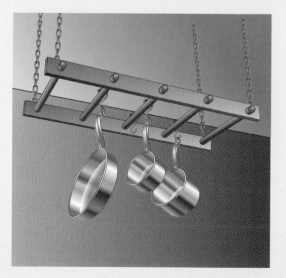

Pot racks most commonly hang over kitchen islands or peninsulas, but they may be suspended over sinks or countertops as well. If you have a high ceiling, they may even be sensibly hung over walk space. When hanging pots, pans, and stovetop cooking utensils, choose a location near your oven range. On the other hand, when hanging items like colanders, bowls, strainers, whisks, and graters, the pot rack should be kept near a prep area.

Exposed pots and pans can help to create a warm, lived-in look in your kitchen.

Plates are stored vertically between the upper and lower cabinet, freeing up cabinet space.

A generously sized center island creates ample room for food prep, allowing the homeowner to keep books, utensils, and appliances on the countertop without feeling pressed for space.

Pantries

If you have more space than just your kitchen to work with, create a pantry that has a wider variety of storage options without sacrificing accessibility.

A pantry is any space that holds perishable, non-perishable, dry, and canned foods. You can annex any adjacent spaces to the kitchen to make a pantry. If you have a closet off of the kitchen, you can turn it into a wonderful walk-in pantry. Or, you can install a shallow built-in or use a standalone hutch wherever you have available space in or near your kitchen.

Drawers make it easy to find and access small items.

A floor-to-ceiling pantry! With this much space, there are plenty of options to make sure that you not only have somewhere to store your food, but that you are able to retrieve it, as well.

Adjustable shelving allows you to customize your storage space.

This pantry makes good use of adjustable shelving that can easily adapt as the needs of your pantry change. Clever produce baskets are also a good choice, as they allow air to circulate freely around perishables.

Stackable containers are a pantry "must." Group containers by the type of food stored within, to make each item easy to find.

When you have more food to store than you know what to do with—and no extra room in your house to store it—it's time to install a mini pantry. In addition to the lazy Susan, there are other ways to customize those same cupboard spaces to fit your food storage needs.

A closet-style mini-pantry with standard shelving can be a good solution for bulk items.

This corner mini pantry features three slide-out drawers for easy access to the deep corner space, while the upper shelves are constructed in a shallow triangle shape so that items don't get lost.

Installing pull-out pantry trays dramatically increases the storage capabilities of a former closet and transforms it into a pantry.

Tip

Whether ordering food by the case at your local co-op or grocer, or stocking up on non-perishables at one of the mega-store discount outlets, buying food in bulk will save you a substantial amount of money in your grocery bills.

If you have wine in your house, it is important to store it well. Any wine stored poorly, even short-term, will almost certainly degrade.

Wines should be kept cool and away from direct sunlight. The optimal temperature range is between 50 degrees and 59 degrees (F). While some variations can be forgiven, there are good reasons for this rule: bottles that freeze will uncork themselves, and wine that reaches 78 degrees (F) will begin to cook, resulting in a loss of quality.

If you store wine for more than a few weeks, store bottles horizontally and in a room with relatively high humidity (about 75 percent). Both of these factors prevent the corks from drying out, which would allow oxygen to reach the wine.

Besides giving a contemporary feel to an ancient pursuit, stainless steel wine racks provide solid construction capable of bearing the weight of many bottles of wine.

Combination horizontal storage and display racks allow plenty of room for proper long-term storage.

If you have the space and your wine collection necessitates it, you may choose to build a basement wine cellar. The dark and cool environment of most basements provides optimal conditions for wine storage. Cellars usually stand within the optimal temperature range and provide a slightly more humid environment, which ensures a long and healthy cork life.

Basement wine cellars also often provide ample space for wine storage along the walls, whether your basement is finished or unfinished. If you are a serious wine connoisseur, you may want to think about building your wine cellar in a finished basement room with a heavy, solid-oak door to help maintain constant temperature in the wine cellar and ensure that the room remains dark. You may also want to create a space for displaying and tasting especially prized bottles or hosting guests.

Bins like these are perfect for storing multiple bottles of the same vintage.

Bathrooms, Linens & Laundry

Remember the old saying that you can never be too rich or too thin? That opinion is—and always has been—debatable, but this much is true: you simply cannot have too much bathroom storage.

Did you know that the average American woman applies 33 products to her face and body each morning before leaving the house? You read that right—thirty-three products. Add the products used by a spouse or partner and a child or two, and you're looking at 40 to 50 containers competing for space in the bathroom. And that's for an average family—high-maintenance folks have an even larger array.

And so we come to the subject of storage, which unleashes a series of questions. How many cabinets do you need, and should they be built-in or freestanding? Closed cabinets or open shelves? Is a pedestal sink workable or do you absolutely need a vanity?

Only you can answer these important questions, but we're here to help. Page through the clever storage throughout this chapter. Take notes about what you find interesting and attractive, then spend some time thinking about your family's habits and routines. The best storage solutions are ones that meet your specific needs and suit your personal taste.

Bathrooms are all about functionality, which presents an inherent storage challenge: How do you create the storage you need so each piece of your daily routine is available where you need it, when you need it? Look for opportunities in your bathroom to build in clever storage, both open and enclosed. With a critical eye, consider all spaces that aren't currently being used and find a way to maximize each space while maintaining order. Because after all, your bathroom should be a relaxing space, where you can put your mind (and your clutter) away quickly and easily.

Well-placed hooks make sure that towels and robes are easily accessible and don't end up on the floor.

Simple, open glass shelving allows light from the windows to filter through the entire room while also taking advantage of valuable vertical storage space.

Even the lip of the bathtub is an opportunity to store frequently-used items.

Vanities are a great way to hide away necessary, but less attractive bathroom musts, such as cleaning products and toilet paper.

Open Storage

Never given much thought to your bathroom walls? You're not alone. Other than old jokes about writing on them, bathroom walls don't get much attention. However, the walls in your bathroom are a great opportunity for storage of everyday necessities that are all-too-often missed.

Words to Know

Cementboard: A substrate used under ceramic tile and stone. Cementboard remains stable even when exposed to moisture, a critical issue in bathrooms.

Fiber/cementboard: A thin, high-density underlayment used in wet areas where floor height is a concern.

Greenboard: Drywall treated to withstand occasional moisture. It's a good choice for bathroom walls outside wet zones.

Drywall: Panels consisting of a gypsum core covered in paper.

Partition walls are often not load-bearing, which makes them a great place for built-in storage, such as the glass shelving shown here. Its transparency helps open up enclosed bathroom spaces, and allows light to easily move through the room. The shelves also provide ample space for storing bath products or extra towels where they are easily accessible by your guests.

A built-in like this can easily be cut into a perimeter wall as well. Just make sure to check that the space is clear of electrical wiring and other utility lines before you start cutting. Also, many bathrooms have specialized wall materials to cope with the excessive moisture and heat often produced in bathrooms (see Words to Know). Make sure you finish the work with appropriate materials and techniques, and always wear respiratory protection.

Put a clever twist on the traditional vanity by installing open shelving below a sink surround. In small spaces, open shelving creates the illusion of extra space and puts all the small items you use every day within quick and easy reach.

The room pictured below also includes built-in medicine cabinets on both sides of a large mirror, which are a great hideaway for toothbrushes and beauty products. These cabinets match the rest of the sink surround perfectly, enabling them to blend in with the rest of the room's décor.

Add a closet rod in front of open shelving to place towels within easy reach without adding additional hardware to the bathroom walls.

Cabinets

Cabinets are not just for kitchens! When it comes to bathroom storage, cabinetry is one of the smartest and most overlooked solutions. Cabinetry has a very long useful life and is likely to remain in place for many years.

If your cabinets work well, but look outdated, consider painting or refacing them. Paint is an option only for wood cabinets, but both wood and laminate cabinets can be refaced by installing new cabinet doors, drawer fronts, and matching veneer on face frames and cabinet ends.

Bathroom cabinets should meet your needs. Consider who uses the bathroom, how, and when, and plan storage that works for your life. Here, a combination of doors, drawers, and open shelves store toiletries and grooming essentials for the two adults who use the room, typically one at a time.

This bathroom is a storage dream. Cabinets, drawers, and open shelving all fit seamlessly in the bathroom's design. Even the space beneath the bench at right is outfitted with cabinet doors. However, because most of the storage in this bathroom is closed, the room maintains an open, relaxing atmosphere.

Words to Know

On framed cabinets, the exposed edges of the cases are covered with flat (face) frames. The doors may be set into the frames or overlay them; the hinges are attached to the frames and the doors. Framed cabinets require more materials but often are less exacting to build than frameless. They are preferable in historic or traditional-style homes.

On frameless cabinets, the exposed edges are covered with edge banding and the doors cover nearly the entire case. The door hinges are attached to the doors and the sides or ends of the cases. Frameless cabinets require less material but can be more time consuming to build than framed. The structure allows for wider doors and better accessibility.

Cabinets do not have to be ornate or even prominent to get the job done. The main goal for storage in a bathroom—or any other room, for that matter—is to keep things near their point of use. Simple. Hair dryers should be housed near mirrors; towels near the shower, tub, and sinks; bubble bath near the tub. You get the idea.

The trick to planning efficient storage is first to figure out what is used and where, then to decide how those things will be stored. Consider placing pull-out shelves and drawers, hampers, and trash cans behind closed doors.

Cabinets painted bright white float into the background of this bathroom's relaxing spa-like atmosphere.

A generously sized tub surround has plenty of space for storing extra towels out in the open.

The space between the sinks is defined here with a tray containing personal items and other toiletries.

Tall cabinets beneath the sinks leaves plenty of space for storage around plumbing.

Extra large drawers are perfect for storing cleaning products and other large items.

Having a place for everything simplifies daily life.

In remodeling projects or new construction, decide on locations and sizes for the towel bars early in the process so blocking can be installed before the drywall is hung.

Teak, a durable hardwood, is at home in moist environments, such as bathrooms. This bench holds clothing and other items while family members bathe, and makes a great place to sit while changing clothes.

Towels, sponges, soaps, and candles are stored where they're used in this relaxed atmosphere.

By the way, if you haven't considered one before, now's the time: a towel warmer may be the ultimate luxury. These days, towel warmers can be found at surprisingly reasonable prices. Some are hard-wired into an available electrical circuit; others simply plug into a receptacle. Either way, you're in for a treat. Who wouldn't love wrapping themselves in a warm, fluffy towel on a cold day?

Transform necessities into accessories by storing them in plain sight.

Large, bulky, or unattractive items are hidden behind closed doors in the vanity cabinets.

Slightly obscured behind textured glass doors, common objects such as a hand mirror, pottery, and towels become decorative pieces in their own right.

Displaying towels attractively isn't exactly fine art, but there is a trick to it. For each stack, fold all the towels in the same manner and to the same size, then stack them with all the folds facing the same direction. This might sound trivial, but try it. Details like this transform ordinary things into extraordinary displays.

Open and Movable Storage

Neatly organized open storage can replace cabinetry in some situations. In this bathroom, the white paneling adds too much character to the bathroom's design to cover up. Instead, white shelves complement the room's clean lines. The tidy shelving adds function and an opportunity for the homeowners to display their personality and interest. The antique camera collection that occupies the top cubbies of these shelving units provides a perfect example of this technique.

Add a Built-in Shelf

It just can't be done: You can never have too much storage in a bathroom. Especially in small bathrooms, take every opportunity to add storage.

Frame an opening into a partition—or non-load-bearing wall—and trim it with window casings.

Have glass shelves cut to fit the opening and install them on small cleats attached to the sides of the opening.

If privacy is an issue, fill the shelves with plants and other decorative items to block the view.

For small bathrooms without storage, often the linen and medicine-cabinet products and toiletries must share a space with laundry in a nearby closet. To keep everything in order and easy to find within shared spaces, stack and label clear storage boxes on an organized shelving system. Keep those items most used on top.

In some rooms, it's possible to add a large, built-in linen closet. This solution makes it easy to tuck away all your essentials, leaving your bathroom spacious and peaceful.

Without cabinetry built in to their bathroom, these homeowners created storage space with clever furniture pieces and built-in wall niches. The result is both functional and attractive.

In a small bathroom like this, transparent cabinet doors preserve the room's sense of space while they conceal bathroom essentials in a handy place.

This attractive, comfortable bathroom has been designed for maximum accessibility and efficiency for everybody, with movable storage and well-planned details.

Glass shelving works double-duty here, as both a decorative element and open storage.

Roll-out base cabinets provide seating space without sacrificing storage.

Bars attached to the front of the countertops allow seated users to pull themselves into position—and hold towels right where they're needed.

Including countertops and sinks at different heights creates accessible space for all users. Comfortable heights range from 32 to 43" for standing users and 30 to 34" for seated users.

A sink can be nestled between stacks of drawers.In drawer stacks like these, store things according to how often you use them—place those used most often in the top drawer, least often in the bottom.

Take advantage of any open space around the sink. Here, a generous storage piece tucked between the sink and tub holds daily supplies and a towel ring for the sink.

Console-table sinks offer no real storage, which can present problems. If you love the style but think you can't sacrifice the storage offered by a vanity, think again. You may have more options than you first realize.

Make sure wood shelving and cabinets are protected by water-resistant finishes.

Tip

Recycle a salvaged upper cabinet into an inexpensive storage and display piece for your bathroom. Choose a cabinet with glass-front doors; if none are available, choose one with raised panel doors and replace the flat panel with glass. If you can find one, an old cabinet from above a refrigerator makes an interesting piece.

If necessary, refinish or repaint the cabinet. Add screw-on legs with leveling devices, and you're all set.

Caution: If a cabinet predates 1978 and has not been refinished, it may have lead paint. Have the piece professionally stripped before you refinish or repaint it. Lead poses serious health hazards and must not be handled casually.

Designers suggest storing towels within 12" of sinks, tubs, and showers. If your bathroom doesn't meet this guideline, fill in with accessories. Here, a simple set of wood shelves stores towels within reach of both the shower and the tub.

Hooks are an attractive place to store jewelry you wear frequently—not only will it be easy to find, your jewelry will also be a part of your bathroom's décor.

Surface-mounted and stand-alone storage accessories may lack the permanence of their built-in counterparts, but they have the advantage of being moved easily as your storage needs evolve. They also have a light, contemporary style.

Storage space is at a premium in bathrooms. Employing some kitchen-style cabinet organizing tricks helps boost efficiency.

Furniture and fixtures can be combined with great effect in any room, but a bathroom is a prime candidate. Here, a small serving sideboard is fitted with a granite countertop and plumbed to support an undermount lavatory sink. Make sure to fasten plumbed furnishings to the wall or floor for stability and safety.

This clever toilet paper dispenser holds multiple rolls so you won't be caught unprepared.

A step stool for the little ones is stored under the sink.

Sink side accessories are kept within reach without occupying cabinet space.

Two cabinets to the left and right of the mirror keep the usual bathroom clutter out of sight while still helping to lighten up the small bathroom footprint. The matching cabinet below the sink is outfitted with shelving to make the space usable for storage.

Wall-mounted lavatory faucets free up countertop space, and they also improve access to vanity cabinet interiors.

Combine open shelving with vanity storage for complete flexibility. The glass shelving installed on the wall above one of the double sinks here is perfect for storing frequently used items. The enclosed vanity conceals less attractive items, while keeping them within quick and easy reach. The combination of cabinets and drawers beneath the sinks is a versatile solution for a wide variety of items.

Also, the raised sink on the left opens up the storage cabinet below even more, as the sink's basin won't impede upon the vertical space of the cabinet.

Mirrors, hooks, baskets, storage pieces—they all contribute to the ambience as well as the efficiency of this eclectic bathroom.

Well-placed hooks make it easy to keep bathrooms neat and organized.

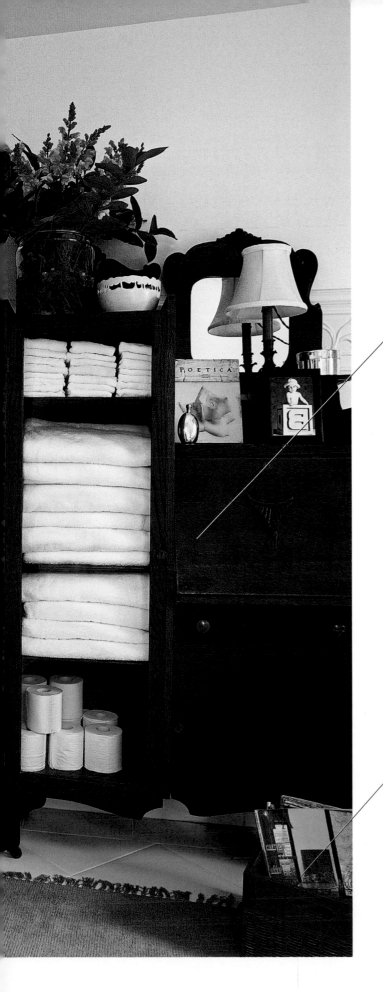

Bathroom accessories simplify daily living.

Antique furniture can double as a makeshift linen closet. This unique piece becomes the bathroom's defining design statement and serves a helpful function.

Baskets keep magazines and other reading material collected and close at hand.

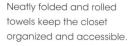

Linen Storage

You can never have enough room for linens. A variety of clean towels and sheets are great to have around, but they take up space, and fast! Linen closets can easily double as storage spaces for extra bed-and-bath necessities.

Store soaps and bath supplies toward the front of shelves, so they won't get lost where they can't be seen or reached.

Neatly folded and rolled towels keep the closet organized and accessible.

Keep bulky pillows and comforters on lower shelves so they are easily accessible.

A linen closet should have room for extra towels and linens for guests. Space shelves to provide enough room to stack folded towels—but not too much room, which leads to clutter and wasted vertical space.

A convenient bench doubles as additional storage space.

This cabinet holds a lot of bathroom essentials without taking up hardly any space. A built-in project like this is perfect for small or extremely busy bathrooms.

When planning for towel storage, it's a good idea to build in space for dirty towels as well as clean ones. The cabinet pictured here cleverly houses a pull-out laundry bin for used towels and washcloths.

Laundry Centers

We all know that there is a direct correlation between the quality of a laundry room space and how much we dread doing the laundry. Cramped, cluttered, or poorly arranged rooms add to the work's unpleasantness. Sometimes, however, all that's needed to transform your laundry center into an efficient and pleasant work center is—you guessed it—plenty of storage.

Wall pockets are a great place to keep dryer sheets, clothespins, specialized detergents, and other small items.

Ample designated space to hang drying clothes is essential to a well-organized laundry center.

A large work surface is a laundry center luxury everyone should have. Use this space to sort, fold, stack, and mend.

Rolling laundry carts help keep the laundry center's mess in check. Sized to be housed underneath a spacious work surface, they exhibit one of the key features of smart storage: they add capacity without impinging on usable floor space.

Make sure you include a closet rod to hang clothes as you're folding laundry.

These small drawers are perfect for storing small items like clothespins, cleaning rags, and simple hand tools.

Cabinets are a smart choice for laundry room storage. This laundry center has enough extra room to store some household utility items like light bulbs, hand tools, and extension cords.

A laundry room is the perfect ally for a mud room. Dirty clothes coming in the door can be thrown right into the hamper. Baskets can house hats and mittens in winter and towels, sandals, and sunscreen lotion in summer.

A folding table is a great
solution if space is tight.

This sunny laundry center has space for everything. Ample cabinets and
shelving, a roll-away folding table, space above the sink for hanging
clothes to dry, even a tall cabinet for linen storage. A system like this
doesn't require more space than the wall behind your washer and dryer,
but has a huge impact on your home's organization.

A hideaway ironing board that folds up into a recessed cabinet is a great convenience and space-saver. Hideaway ironing boards can either be built in between wall studs or mounted on the wall's surface.

Bright wall and stair colors help to liven up this basement laundry center. Matching baskets on overhead shelves tame linens and other storage items, and the large, open shelves are a perfect place to keep blankets, detergents, and other essentials.

Family &
Entertainment
Rooms

Family and entertainment rooms are the hardest working rooms in your home. These multi-purpose living spaces are where the family gathers to relax—so they should be practical, comfortable, inviting rooms that encourage interaction and fun.

Every family's unique lifestyle and hobbies will present different storage challenges for common living areas. If your family frequently gathers to watch movies or listen to music, practical and organized media storage may be your primary concern. Or perhaps your living room doubles as a library or showroom for family artifacts, and you'd like to find creative ways to store books and other objects. It's most likely, however, that many different kinds of activities take place in your family room, in which case you're probably looking for clever ways to hide away all kinds of objects, from throw blankets to remote controls to board games. This chapter includes plenty of ideas to help you do just that.

Also included in this chapter are ideas for how best to maximize storage in the transitional spaces of your home—entryways, hallways, stairways, and other nooks and crannies. Building in smart storage space in your home's most high-traffic areas is a great first step toward creating a tidy, comfortable space for you and your family to hang out, relax, and be together.

Family Rooms

In family rooms with an entertainment center, creating appropriate storage for your audio/visual equipment and media is a major concern. At the low end there are ready-to-assemble (RTA) modular shelving systems or manufactured stand-alone units that can meet your basic needs. Many of these options, however, are disappointing to style-conscious consumers.

In this basement family room, a large custom built-in provides the perfect backdrop for an entertainment center—keeping all wires out of sight and everything organized and within reach. The cabinet doors near the TV are on a pivot door slide so they either conceal the TV or slide out of the way when the TV is in use.

Living room furniture with built-in shelving, such as the coffee table shown here, is a great choice. The bottom shelf is the perfect place to keep books, magazines, remote controls, and other frequently used items.

Adding lighting to open storage in a built-in unit is a great way to add warmth and depth to a living space, and it helps to showcase collectible items and artifacts.

Benches double as storage for firewood or media.

This comfortable space is the perfect mix of enclosed and open storage. The built-in drawers and cabinets are a great place to hide away unattractive items, whereas bookshelves and mantels showcase family artifacts, books, and games within easy reach. The combination of the two gives the room a lived-in, but tidy feel.

Although modern design can present a storage challenge for living spaces, building in storage is still very possible with a little creativity. This contemporary living room is organized into two cozy sitting areas around a sizeable earth-tone fireplace near the center of the room.

Every element is well considered here to create the bright, contemporary look of the space. Storage areas are camouflaged all around the room, and blend seamlessly into the clean linear design. The bookshelf along the wall is perhaps the best example. Although the shelf appears to be made up entirely of open storage for showcasing books, lamps, and other decorative items, notice that the bottom shelf of the unit utilizes translucent doors, perfect for concealing other items. The central coffee table can hold a limited number of high-interest items, whereas the built-in bookshelf behind the fireplace can hold an immense amount of books and other items—conveniently located, but just out of the way of the room's more prominent design features.

Translucent doors conceal stored items without affecting the room's clean, contemporary appearance.

This living space combines drawers with shelving around the entertainment center for maximum media storage.

Books and magazines are stacked according to size, which gives these shelves a more organized appearance.

In just over 100 years, we have seen a dizzying variety of home audio and video formats that have been championed and then abandoned, from vinyl records and 8-tracks to CDs and now mp3s, as well as Super-8 home movies to the advent of VHS, DVD, and Blu-ray. To support all these formats, we collect a lot of devices, players, cords, plugs, cables, and appliances that allow us to enjoy them.

To accommodate the sheer volume of materials you'll no doubt acquire, built-in cabinets and storage space can provide flexibility and accessibility without eating up all your floor space.

Cabinet doors keep electronic components and cables hidden when not in use.

Deep drawers make use of cabinet depth for keeping media orderly and accessible without taking up more flat wall space.

Projector screens rival flat LCD screens for portability. Unlike LCD screens, a projection screen can be rolled up when not in use.

In today's homes, the TV room may also need to be the living room, the family room, or the den. This is made easier with cabinets that hide and protect the television when it is not in use.

This combination entertainment center and bookcase offers sturdy platform-style shelving and ample television space. The television is large enough to be seen from the kitchen island, which opens to the living room in the lower right corner of this photo. The plain-faced wood sliding panels can be moved to cover either the television or the books.

Where's the TV? Clearly, it and the rest of the entertainment system can be found within the large modular cabinets mounted to the back wall. Because modular cabinets can appear bulky and weigh down a room, the homeowner painted, added decorative hardware, and mounted these stock cabinets into custom-built alcoves to create a warm backdrop for the room when the entertainment system is not in use.

It's not often you see a television on the mantel! Here, the television is concealed behind hinged doors so as not to draw attention away from the wraparound library. The simple facade of the lower cabinets and drawers gives the room a classic style.

There are a variety of shelving systems available that are less expensive and easier to reconfigure than custom built-in storage. As your media collection grows in shape, size, and format, you can add or replace standalone pieces as needed. A well-chosen standalone piece can complement existing built-ins nicely.

Wicker baskets are a versatile way to store vinyl, CDs, or DVDs. They substitute a warm earth tone for a row of messy media spines and can be picked up and rifled through while you're sitting on the couch.

Modular shelving makes expanding a home entertainment center simple. Most systems are adjustable and come in standard styles so complementary pieces can be added when necessary.

This simple, spare, metal design illustrates that inexpensive track shelving can look stylish and modern. This clever homeowner installed the system in a reach-in closet with a sliding door, allowing the system to be hidden from view when not in use.

Some creative tile work can convert unsightly media storage into a lovely conversation starter in your media room.

Media Collections

If you collect music, movies, or video games, an efficient means to store them is a must. With a system that is easy to use, you'll be more inclined to put everything back in its place, making it easier to find things again later. And if your system doesn't have space to grow as your collection grows, the problem of losing or misplacing things is almost inevitable. You may have already found this to be true.

Thankfully, there are countless storage options, so don't settle. Even on a tight budget, you can find interesting storage that will fit your decor. There are models that sit on the floor, on shelves, hang over doors, mount to walls, or hang from ceilings—all in styles ranging from modern to baroque. Media storage is such a pervasive issue in the modern world that if you can dream of it, you can probably find it for sale.

Media storage doesn't have to take up much,
or any, floor space. Slotted shelving for CDs is trim,
compact, and doesn't take up much more space
than the CDs themselves.

Discarding CD jewel cases and keeping only the discs and artwork allows you to carry four times as much music in the same amount of space. Vinyl-sleeve systems preserve everything that came with the jewel case. Sleeves are more durable than jewel cases—there are no hinges to break and the heavy-duty vinyl won't tear. An ATA-approved flight case holds 300 CD sleeves, takes up very little space, and is virtually indestructible.

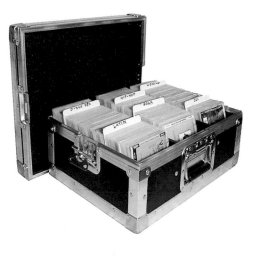

Tip

Tired of losing track of your remote controls? Rather than buying an expensive "remote control caddie" or universal controller, purchase a simple and inexpensive wicker or other decorative basket that can sit on a coffee table, end table, or even right on the couch. If an item has a designated storage space, you and your family will be more inclined to put it back there when you're through using it.

A roll-away box is perfect for storing video game consoles, controllers, cords, and games.

If you are a music lover, how to store multiple kinds of media and electronic equipment in an organized, easily accessible way is probably pretty high on your list of priorities. The options available to you are nearly limitless, so make sure that the storage system you choose truly meets your needs and protects the items that are the most important to you (see page 86).

A music listening room is separated from a home office by a striated glass wall. This gesture provides some privacy and diffused light while not closing off the space with an opaque wall. Separating two spaces that are both used to store and organize information and materials is a great way to help you maintain different organizational systems. Always make sure to store items in the space where you use them the most.

Good listening rooms often follow the "rule of eight"—that is, your speakers should stand eight-feet apart with your listening position eight feet back, forming a triangle. While this is a good standard, be careful not to separate your speakers too wide apart for the space, as the sound may then suffer a "hole in the middle" effect.

To maintain good sound quality a listening room should contain a variety of materials so that it is neither too "hard" nor too "soft." Similarly, the ceiling and floor should be of opposite reflectivity. If the floor is absorptive (e.g., carpeting) the ceiling should be hard (e.g., drywall), and vice-versa. Also, arrange furniture, record racks, and other elements, somewhat evenly around the room to break up the sound reflections caused by parallel planes.

Archiving Media at Home

General media storage

Films, photos, tapes, and digital media don't last forever, especially if they're improperly stored. Most media will last far longer if kept clean, cool, and dry—that's under 70 degrees (F), with relative humidity between 30 and 50 percent.

Attics are often too hot and dry, basements and garages too cold and damp—but closets close to the center of the house, or even the space under a bed, can be convenient and stable storage environments.

Avoid shelves close to the ceiling, which can get much hotter than eye-level storage, and may also be susceptible to a leaking roof.

Never store important materials in direct sunlight. Sunlight fades photographs and printed materials, and can turn storage boxes into small ovens. If you have vintage photos hanging where they're exposed to daylight, consider reframing them with UV-filtering glass, or even moving them elsewhere.

Stable storage conditions are almost as important as ones that fall within the appropriate temperature and humidity. If you find a place in your home that's a degree or two warmer than recommended, but it's the same temperature and humidity year-round, that's better than a spot that gets exposed to frequent spikes in heat or humidity.

Plastic containers are a mixed blessing. They can offer inexpensive, sturdy, and dust-proof storage; however, they can also seal in harmful humidity and damaging chemicals. If used, plastic containers should be made of inert materials (polyester, polyethylene, or polypropylene), and vented to allow air circulation.

Photographs

Family pictures are high on the list of things people say they'd save if their house was on fire. Why not take a few simple steps now to prevent them from being damaged in other ways?

The bleach and acids used in manufacturing regular paper can discolor or destroy photographs. Acid-free envelopes, folders, boxes, and albums are the archivist's choice for storing valuable documents and pictures, and they should be yours, too.

Photographic negatives should be removed from acidic glassine envelopes and stored in opaque containers, away from any sources of light. Try to handle negatives as little as possible—you can always make new prints, but negatives are irreplaceable!

Those old photo albums with sticky pages and plastic overlays are terrible for pictures over the long term. Transfer them to an acid-free album.

Films

Old home movies are a great way for each new generation to get to know the family history. Taking care of your family films makes it easy—and fun—to travel back in time to grandma's wedding, dad's first birthday, or Uncle Joe's trip to the World's Fair.

Film is made of organic materials and can decay rapidly if sealed in a very warm or humid environment.

Store film in vented, inert plastic cans or acid-free boxes and check it regularly for signs of deterioration. These are easy to spot—stable film should lie flat, unwind easily from the reel, and have no unpleasant odor. Film that's in trouble may be stuck together, smell like vinegar, or show white mold crystals on the outside edges. Separate any damaged or decaying film from other materials immediately, since mold and vinegar syndrome can spread to the rest of your collection.

If you rehouse your films before storing them, be sure to photocopy any notes from the original cans or boxes. They can provide valuable clues about hard-to-identify locations, events, or participants.

Video and audiotapes

Whether it's home movies or Hollywood films, the tapes in your personal video library will all last longer if they're stored properly.

Make sure all tapes—especially home movies—have clear, legible labels describing their current contents. This will save you time when searching for that school play or graduation ceremony.

Lint and dust particles are especially harmful to the delicate tape inside videocassettes; always keep videotapes in their cases.

Tapes should be kept as cool and dry as possible. If you don't have storage room in a cool, dry cabinet, think creatively: stack tapes two or three high in a flat, acid-free box with a lid and tuck it away under the couch or coffee table.

Digital media

Remember the floppy disks that were actually floppy? Those were state of the art 25 years ago, and now you'd be hard-pressed to find a computer that could even read one, let alone the software we used back then. And unlike films and photographs, the contents of digital media can't be read from the outside. These factors make proper storage of digital media especially crucial.

Label diskettes, CD-Rs, DVDs, and other storage devices clearly and completely. Keep a printed index of the files stored on each disk, too, including the version of the software program used to create each file.

Keep up with changing technologies! When you upgrade your computer, or get a new kind of storage drive, always make sure you can access all of your old data with the new system. Migrate and back up the contents of your digital archive to the newest storage medium you use, and spot-check enough of your imported or migrated files to be sure that any new software is backward compatible (capable of reading files created with older versions).

Diskettes are magnetic media, and should be kept in non-ferrous-metal containers, away from magnets or strong electrical fields. CDs and DVDs are optical media, so magnets won't harm them. All digital media should be kept free from dust, heat, and humidity.

Home Theaters

The fastest growing trend in home design is the inclusion of a home theater. Advances in LCD displays, projectors, speakers, and high definition technology have made high quality home theater environments affordable to more people than ever before. Home theaters, of course, can still cost thousands of dollars, but a good entry-level system including a big screen (30 inches or larger) or projection television, speakers, and a surround sound capable receiver can be produced for under $5,000; a bare-bones system can be assembled for as little as $2,000. The space designed to maximize the potential of this technology will add its own costs as well, but unlike the electronics, the room itself will add value to your home at time of resale.

In most houses, the best location for a home theater is the basement. This is because it is, obviously, much easier to block out light in basements for a theater-like effect, but it's also easier to insulate basements for sound than rooms on the main floor. And after all, controlling light and sound is what the home theater experience is all about.

Front-projection televisions offer the advantage of retractable screens that disappear from view when not in use.

There are essentially three types of television screens in today's consumer market: the original direct view CRT (cathrode ray tube) television, flat panels (e.g, LCD, plasma, and OLED monitors), and front- and rear-projection televisions.

They each have their advantages and disadvantages. The front-projection television shown here is unique, however, in that it is the only viewing option where you find yourself within the image environment rather than in front of it. In the industry, they say that the viewer is placed "inside the box" a condition which some argue offers the most intimate viewing experience of any home theater system.

Video projector technology, whether front or rear, comes in a few styles: CRT (cathode ray tube), DLP (digital light processing), and LCD (liquid crystal display).

Home Libraries

These days, it is rare to find a house with a separate, formal library. Perhaps, in an era of compact media and large televisions, it's a blessing that bookshelves are integrated throughout the home, where they are on display as we go through our everyday lives.

A combination dining room and library: perfect for hosting the book club. Even with shelves built in from floor to ceiling all around the room, subtle lighting can change the room from imposing and magisterial to inviting and warm.

A wall of dark-stained built-in bookshelves around a fireplace creates the feeling of a classic home library.

Rooms with high or vaulted ceilings can hold bookshelves much taller than most people can reach without a ladder.

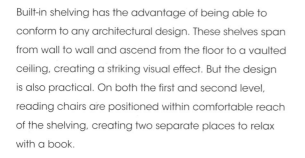

Built-in shelving has the advantage of being able to conform to any architectural design. These shelves span from wall to wall and ascend from the floor to a vaulted ceiling, creating a striking visual effect. But the design is also practical. On both the first and second level, reading chairs are positioned within comfortable reach of the shelving, creating two separate places to relax with a book.

Bring more visual interest to shelving by mixing photographs, vases, and magazines in with your books.

Resting books on their side can break up the monotony and act as bookends.

There are many freestanding bookshelves available at home centers and furnishings retailers. These lightweight, leaning shelves provide plenty of space in a very small footprint. The open back keeps smaller rooms from feeling boxed in.

Many modular shelving systems are so well configured to fit the style and size of a room that they emulate built-ins.

The best shelving is adjustable, providing flexibility for future storage needs.

Modular lighting affixed to the top of the shelving draws attention to the display items on the shelves, making it easier for you to find the book you're looking for.

Freestanding modular shelving can do more than fade into the background. Some interesting designs can make nearly anything look better.

Glass shelves draw emphasis to "showcase" objects and help lighten the imposing appearance of the weighty component.

The triangular corner allows for a varied collection of earthenware to grace the entrance to the room, rather than the flat exterior of a bookcase.

If you can find shelving that encourages you to display interesting objects while being an interesting structural component in its own right, so much the better. The dark finish contrasts nicely with the light wall color, helping this built-in component anchor the room without dominating the space.

Not all bookshelves must be shoved up against the wall of a room. Putting an open-backed unit out in the open can nicely partition a room, while becoming an aesthetic object itself.

Freestanding, open shelving can make expansive spaces feel a little less imposing.

The placement of these shelves reduces the extrawide hallway to two human-scaled passageways, one on each side.

Decorative Storage

It is tempting, when you have books or other collectibles piled on the floor, to run out and get the first shelving you find that will manage to contain the items you want to display—just to get them out from underfoot.

But storage doesn't have to be just functional and prosaic. It, too, can be part of the display. Shelving or display tables can be bought or custom made in nearly any material, in nearly any shape! Glass, chrome, steel, copper pipe, brick, pine, oak, fir, mahogany, bamboo, fiberglass, plastic—even custom-formed cement. If you have prized and interesting possessions, you might want to take the time to find the right way to display them. Your mundane objects and shelving can then be left safely behind closed doors.

These galvanized cubes, like most modular cube storage, are the perfect size to house your old record collection.

Galvanized steel can brighten up any room. Consider using individual cubes or similarly sized buckets for holding stray items like toys, magazines, newspapers, or knitting supplies.

Stackable cubes made of any material make versatile and portable modular shelving. This type of storage is a particularly good choice for students or young professionals often on the move.

An unused window with glass shelving installed can serve as a stunning display cabinet. Glass shelving, when backlit, sends a patina of light and color across a room—more dramatic than one might expect from a few simple sheets of glass.

This two-sided unit creates an expansive sense of space as it stores books, wine, and collectibles.

Most homes are not short on wall space. Even with very tight floor space, you can make the most of your display opportunities nearly anywhere in your house by using the walls to their full advantage.

There is a common tendency to mount or hang items, such as shelving or wall-mounted collectibles, too high on the wall. Most display items should be at eye level. If you have several items of differing sizes, mount the largest one at eye level first to act as an anchor, then play with the smaller ones until the arrangement feels right. Arranging items of identical size vertically often looks better than horizontally, and odd numbers of items usually look better than even numbers.

A shallow, custom-built bookcase is a great place to store and display artwork, memorabilia, plants, and—of course—books.

Barely deeper than an ornate picture frame, this ultrashallow hutch unit creates a classic-looking storage solution for pottery, china, and glassware, yet uses less than 6" of floor space.

Locating Wall Studs

To mount heavy items for display, you'll need to set an appropriately sized nail or screw into a wall stud. How do you find a stud in a finished wall, you ask?

The easiest method is to use an electronic studfinder. This relatively inexpensive device uses sonic waves to locate the edges of framing members behind wall and ceiling surfaces.

If you don't have a studfinder, there are a number of other approaches:

• Tap along the wall until you hear the sound change from hollow to dull. The dull spot is the location of a stud. If you're not sure, tap a thin finish nail into the wall—it will push easily through plaster or drywall, but not through a wood stud.

• Look along trim moldings for nails; they indicate framing locations.

• Locate wall receptacles; they typically are attached alongside studs.

• Look for visible drywall seams and popped fasteners, which indicate studs and joists.

And remember: wall studs are spaced 16" on-center in standard home construction.

Halls & Stairways

Transitional spaces are not only an opportunity to show off your favorite things, they are also a great opportunity to store items in volume without letting them invade your living areas. Think critically about the passageways in your home to see if you could potentially be using them more effectively to store and organize living-area clutter.

Shallow cabinets installed along a hallway or living room create much-needed pantry space for earthenware storage without sacrificing the elegant look of the home.

Glazed French doors and decorative molding invite attention to this display shelving, but a concealed pantry—which is far less expensive—could work just as well.

The walls near a spiral staircase are a perfect place to build in book or media storage.

A spiral staircase is a great choice for small spaces, as it really helps to free up floor space.

Built-in shelving on a landing can be the perfect out-of-the-way spot for a home library.

A hallway doesn't have to be a vacant passageway on your way to somewhere else. With a little care and planning, a hallway can become a place to linger and to appreciate on its own terms.

It can be difficult to use a hallway well. You may not have great natural light or a roomy floor plan, but you have wall space, which may be enough room for a small table or display shelving. Well-chosen lighting can highlight wall hangings.

Stand in your hallway and look at it, and then, look out of it. What catches your eye? Or, what could?

The placement of artwork in the living room maximizes its visibility, even from the far end of this hall. The narrow sculpture in the foreground stands near the hall entrance, but does not crowd it.

The wall space is ample enough in this stairway for several large pictures, and for a large backlit artwork over a display shelf at the landing.

Boxes, baskets, or bowls placed underneath a table can ground a table that might otherwise feel top-heavy and provide a clever storage opportunity.

A table well considered to its space can provide an elegant platform to display a few prized possessions. It's usually best not to crowd a table with too many items; doing so dilutes the visual impact of each individual piece.

Cabinets built in to match the pitch of a staircase are both
a smart storage solution and a striking design element.

Built-in shelving is a natural
fit underneath many
staircases—wine racks for
some, display or library
shelving for others.

If you're looking for something more adaptable and less expensive than built-in shelving, wire racks and baskets will fit nicely beneath many staircases.

Insider Advice: Tricks from the Pros

Judy Colvin, Professional Organizer
J. Colvin Consulting, Sacramento, CA

Unexpected places around the home are waiting for you to expand storage options and help you organize everyday life.

Go Vertical: Wall surfaces stretching from floor to ceiling offer storage space for narrow rooms, closets, and hallways.

• Frame bookcases or other shelving units around a window or a doorway that meets a corner.
• Carve a built-in cabinet, shelf, or closet into a non-structural wall to avoid the need to purchase furniture that would otherwise take up floor space.

Underneath it all: Usable storage exists in places you cannot see.
• Place storage baskets underneath an entryway table or sofa table to create a temporary parking place for incoming/outgoing mail and packages.
• Take advantage of unused space between shelves by installing under-shelf wire baskets or slide-out drawers for frequently used items like sponges, kitchen or bath linens, toiletries, etc.

Behind the Scenes: Empty spaces behind doors offer easy access to everyday items.
• Install door- or wall-mounted organizing accessories to maximize the space behind kitchen/bath cabinet doors, pantry and laundry room doors, etc.
• Stack old-fashioned travel suitcases or large decorative storage boxes behind a sofa to store pillows, blankets, and seasonal outerwear.

Coatrooms & Entries

The first pit stop upon entering the home, the entry closet, is a notorious example of poorly used closet space: overstuffed with out-of-season coats, balled-up mittens, scarves, hats, lonely shoes with no partners, and a top shelf overloaded with board games. What are those doing there?

Wire baskets provide easy access for loose items such as mittens and hats, or sports equipment.

Additional hooks along the adjacent wall offer guests a place to hang their hat.

Plenty of shelving is available for pullovers and sweaters.

This open entryway allows plenty of space for a practical modular storage system. To accommodate the volume of jackets and coats, multiple closet rods make efficient use of the available space—a single rod would have had to span the entire wall. With adequate shelving in place, the floor can be used to keep track of shoes and boots.

However, the entryway to your home is the most important place to get storage right. If you have a place to put down everything you have in your hands when you come in the door, you can avoid bringing things into your home and plopping them down in your living space, a practice which breeds clutter. Remember: a place for everything, everything in its right place.

One way to organize your entryway is to assign each family member a dedicated area within the larger storage unit for his or her "stuff." Because first impressions count, make sure your entry storage is attractive as well as functional.

Cubbies of different sizes are perfect for accommodating items of varying sizes.

A bench is not only a convenient place to sit while you put on or take off shoes, it's also a great opportunity to build in enclosed storage.

A multipurpose storage and information system near your home's main entrance helps manage everything and everyone coming in and going out. And with this system, you don't need a dedicated mudroom space—any wall area near the most-used entry door will do.

A dry erase and bulletin board fit well into the storage system and convert into a quick message center to keep your family in touch.

Wall-mounted filing bins typically used in offices are a wonderful mail-sorting solution for entry areas.

Cubes can be custom built or purchased in a variety of colors and sizes.

Walk-in Closets

A spacious walk-in closet is the envy of all, and for good reason. Not only is a well-organized and functional closet convenient, it can have a substantial effect on your quality of life as well. Imagine workday mornings free of the frantic dig through compact drawers and cramped closets. Alleviating that daily stress not only saves you time, it helps you conserve energy—energy you can use to plan your "alternate route" options for the morning commute.

Multiple closet rods at varying levels can more than double your storage space.

Small cubbies are perfect for shoes or other accessories.

Even Organized Closets Need Regular Attention

Try this time limit test for clothing: Face all of your hanging clothes in one direction. Each time you wear an item, hang it back up in the opposite diretion. After a few months, consider donating all items that are still facing in the original direction.

With a walk-in closet of this size, you'll spend a significant amount of time in it every day. Why not make it a pleasant experience? Everything is arranged where it can be seen, with enough room to access clothes and keep them from getting wrinkled and high storage for infrequently used items.

Adjustable shelving allows you to change your shelving to adapt to your needs.

High shelving is perfect for out-of-season clothing or infrequently used items.

The storage capacity of a closet equipped with one closet rod can be nearly doubled with the installation of a second rod. Remember to leave some full-length hang space for coats, dresses, and long skirts.

If you have sufficient ceiling height, some amount of ambition, and quite a bit of clothing, consider installing three rails or extra-tall shelving and adding a library ladder to make the upper space accessible.

Install high shelves for oversized items or items you don't need on a regular basis.

Separate shoe racks keep the floor clear of clutter.

A combination of shelves, drawers, and closet rods at varying heights make organizing a lot of clothing simple.

Large walk-in closets should be pleasant, organized spaces where everything has a place. Keeping your closet neat and organized will ensure that your everyday life takes on that same trend.

If there are high spaces you need to access regularly, consider including a library ladder in your closet's design.

With floor-to-ceiling storage for clothing, plenty of drawer space, and room for shoes, this closet has room for a dizzying array of outfits. The three clothing rods stacked atop one another put the ample vertical space to good use.

In tight spaces, a mirror can help create the illusion of space. It also allows you to check your appearance before heading out the door.

Closets are also a great place to store accessories, such as neckties or jewelry. Many modular systems include components that integrate accessory organization into the closet design.

A skylight or sun tunnel can add much-needed light to your closet—a space that is traditionally dark and cramped. Improvements in protective coatings for skylights help keep fabrics from fading, but it is still best to design your closet to keep clothing out of direct sunlight.

This custom-bu
storage, and th
comforting ton

Use the varying heights of
your closet rods to help you
separate casual wear from
formal wear.

Walk-in closets can also be a great place to store extra
blankets, pillows, and out-of-season clothing. Look to the upper
shelves of a modular unit like this for ample opportunity to store
these kinds of items.

A freestanding wardrobe is great on its own in a room without a closet or as the perfect adjunct to an existing closet.

While effic
absolute n
is 73 to 78
ceiling, the
    Thankfu
closet's sto
traditional,
shelving to
system allo
finding a r

This wardrobe, with its glass doors and linen interior curtains, mimics the decor of the room to create harmony within the space.

A narrow, freestanding wardrobe can fit in places many closets can't and can be designed to keep your room light and spacious.

Frosted glass doors, recessed lighting, and minimal decoration give this modular wardrobe the appearance of a built-in cabinet.

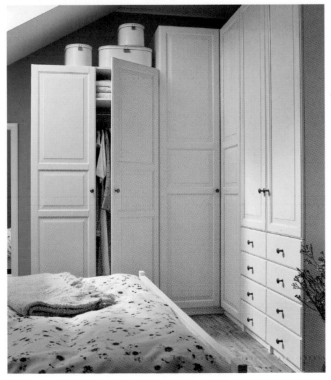

Modular freestanding closets can be arranged and adjusted to fit the size and style of almost any bedroom.

In homes with extremely limited or no closet space, creating closets in the open may be necessary. This closet system, installed along a wall near the sleeping area of a loft apartment, transforms into a bookcase as you move toward the living areas.

Build a Closet Organizer

One of the best ways to maximize the capacity of a closet is to install an organizer that is tailored to your specific storage needs. You can build an organizer for a standard-sized closet for the cost of a single sheet of plywood, a closet rod, and a few feet of 1 × 3 lumber.

Cut the 1 × 3 shelf supports to fit the dimensions of the closet and anchor them to the wall studs at 76 and 84" above the floor. Measure and cut the shelf sides and shelves to size, then assemble the central unit, spacing the shelves according to the height of items you want to store. Measure and cut the upper shelves to size, then fasten the shelves to the wall supports. Finally, install the closet rod as directed by the manufacturer.

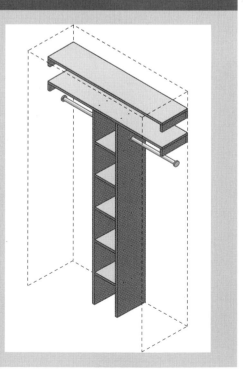

Closed portable storage is the perfect solution to a variety of situations. A fully enclosed, portable closet can make moving far less troublesome—you'll hardly need to unpack. And since closed portable storage keeps clothes dust-free, it's also perfect for storing out-of-season clothing in the basement or attic. It can also offer serviceable additional storage if you're hosting travelers and need some extra space.

Inexpensive organizers are easily available at retail stores or online; more expensive and durable storage is also available for people who will be using it regularly and heavily.

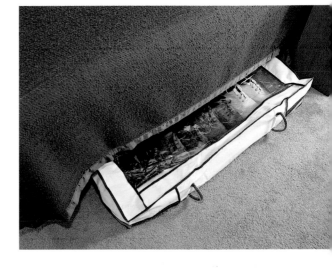

Shoes can easily be stored in flat, closed containers that are easy to pull out or hide away.

This versatile "closet-in-a-box" is made of canvas on a metal frame. Set on wheels, it includes everything: a wardrobe hanger, shelving, drawers, boxes, and a shoe bag.

Open, portable closets challenge our conception of what a closet is. They are not as good for long-term storage as a closed, portable system because they leave their contents vulnerable to dust. For daily use, they are less expensive, far more convenient, and more attractive than most closed, portable closets.

Laundry rooms can benefit from the addition of an open, portable closet to hang wrinkle-free clothes, or to hang dry clothes until they're ready to be put away. Such closets are also an inexpensive option for dorm rooms or small apartments.

An over-the-door hanging-clothes rack provides quick and easy storage space whenever you need it.

Instantly transform a hallway into a coat closet for parties. There are many closet stands on the market that lean against any wall without mounting hardware.

A rolling clothes rack offers extra hanging space at a budget price.

A clothes butler makes dressing in the morning a cinch. In a guest room, a clothes butler may be all the closet space you'll need. It can be rolled aside or collapsed between uses.

Build a Flying Closet

If you're looking for more closet space but don't have room to build, consider installing a "flying closet." Simply purchase a decorative hanging pot rack or set of closet rods. Secure eye-hooks with ¼" thread diameter to the ceiling joists in a corner of the room and hang the flying closet from them with a medium density chain. Use a folding shade or screen to conceal the closet or to create a dressing area.

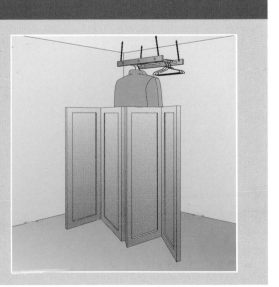

Bedroom suites combine open storage with built-in components to create a living space that transcends easy definition. A large attic is a great candidate to become a suite, as the structure of attics provides ample storage opportunities. Although the remodeling costs could be high, the vast majority (if not all) of the costs will likely be recouped at resale.

These homeowners have transformed the entire wall along the gable side of the attic into custom storage. In addition to the two dresser units, the windowseat conceals storage below.

The matching built-in cabinets and knee wall serve the dual purpose of hiding ductwork and providing storage. Knee wall cabinets are surprisingly deep, and can hold a vast amount of clothing or other items.

Conveniently located wall-mounted fixtures keep the bathroom mess from impeding on the living area.

Learn how to maximize every available storage opportunity. Here, in place of a traditional railing or partial wall, the homeowners have installed an open bookshelf. Notice also the multiple hooks for robes, towel bars, and baskets stored high above the bathroom fixtures.

Open or transitional spaces can double as bedrooms or guest rooms with some careful thought to how you partition the space. In non-traditional bedrooms, always build in storage wherever you can. Look to the walls and to creative furniture choices for the biggest storage impact in a small space.

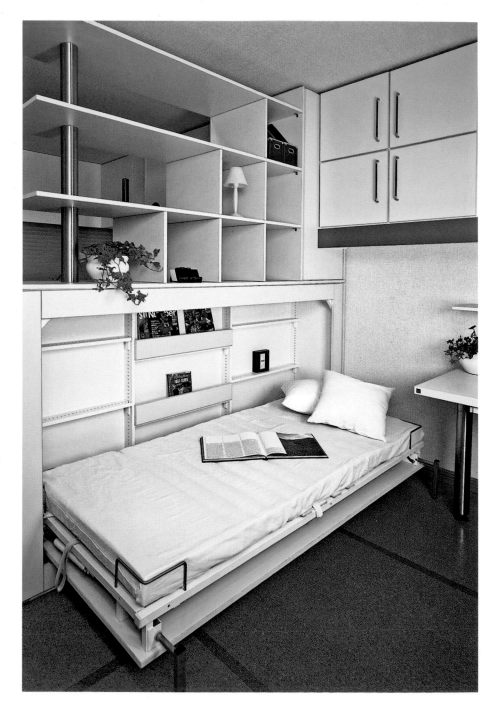

For especially small rooms, or rooms that have multiple uses, consider a Murphy bed, which disappears fully into the wall when not in use. The Murphy bed frees up floor space and allows the room to be fully used during other parts of the day. Notice, also, how the designers of this transitional space used overhead wall storage and modular cubes to make the most of a small space.

In this multi-use space, traditional storage space is hard
to find. The designers of this room make good use of wall
shelving and furniture to store away necessary items.
Installing lighting and translucent doors on furniture pieces
keeps them from looking too bulky in tight spaces.

Get Creative

At the risk of stating the obvious, the real distinguishing feature of a bedroom is a bed. A box spring and mattress take up a lot of floor space, so if you're searching for some extra storage, you'll find it right there, under your bed.

Casters make under-bed bins far easier to access and keep floors from being scratched.

There are many open and closed storage chests, bins, and boxes on the market today that are designed for under-bed storage. From the lavish to simple plastic containers, there's something for any budget. Great for kids' toys or out-of-season storage.

Built-ins under the bed have the advantage of keeping dust bunnies from accumulating and, if equipped with quality drawer slides, are easier to use than modular under-bed storage.

Tip

Instead of buying specialized drawers for under-bed storage, use flat, clear plastic storage boxes to store seasonal clothing, shoes, outerwear, and handbags under the bed. Or convert drawers from an old dresser into new pullout drawers with casters.

Recycle cabinets as a clever bed-surround that doubles as additional storage space. A feature like this both defines the space and frames your room's artwork and wall color.

Underneath isn't the only good place in or around the bed to locate creative storage. Often the bed surround or headboard can also present storage opportunities. You can either purchase premade units or custom build them from existing cabinetry.

A bed surround occupying an entire wall has a dramatic design impact on a room while offering up plenty of storage for a minimal sacrifice of floor space. You can use stock cabinets to build your own surround or have a custom unit built for you. Consider incorporating a reading light or two into the design.

Don't forget that storage can be incorporated into your bed frame. A unit like this could be custom built, or you can purchase a similar piece at local furniture retailers.

Although storage in a kid's room traditionally means "big pile on the floor," here are some interesting and fun ways to make good use of the space. The better the storage is set up, the easier it will be for kids to put their things away when it's clean-up time.

Stairs leading up to an elevated bed double as easy-to-reach storage space. Putting toys away doesn't get any easier than this. A built-in dresser at the foot of the bed isn't a bad idea, either.

An abundance of cabinets, bins, and cubbies are the best way to handle the natural mess of kids' play. Make sure storage is easy for kids to reach—that will ensure it gets used!

The arch on the end of the desk holds display shelving on the exterior and bookshelves in its interior.

This partition wall creates a neat space for built-in display shelving.

Since kids' furniture can look as whimsical or fantastical as a parent can endure, there are not many rules for storage, either.

Seating is amazingly versatile. In an airplane, your seat may store a multimedia controller, a flotation device, and the carry-on baggage of the passenger behind you. At home, your seat can be decorative, multi-functional furniture that also stores a lot of stuff.

A window seat in a child's room creates a sunny retreat for reading and napping, and provides extra storage for toys, clothes, or blankets.

Open, accessible storage in children's rooms should be proportional to their sizes in order for kids to feel comfortable. Try to imagine how things would look from a kid's perspective. Would it be easy for him or her to put things away? Try to make it as convenient as possible for them to put their own toys away, rather than convenient for you to put their toys away for them.

Bright colors and accessible, open shelving for toys will draw the attention of any child.

Create a Gallery for Children's Art

If you have children, you know that finding the right place and the right way to curate your children's art is a perennial issue. To keep your home tidy, create a single gallery space to display the young artist's work. Many parents find that doing so instills in their child a sense of ownership and pride in that area of the house, which often helps to produce a few young tour guides as well as budding artists.

If possible, find a location near their room—a portion of the hallway is ideal. Hang two wires or strings along the wall, one high and one low. Use laundry pins to clip the artwork in place.

Make a rule that for each new masterpiece that goes up, one must come down. And make sure that the child always makes the decision. They'll know if you took something down without conferring with them. And, as you are probably aware, artists are famously temperamental.

Home Offices

Chapter 6

Home offices are becoming a staple in American homes more and more every year. Some of us want a dedicated space just to manage daily household tasks such as paying bills, catching up on emails, or doing homework. There are also more and more professionals all the time who work from the comfort of their home. And, as gas prices increase and businesses continually hone their focus on environmental responsibility, the number of telecommuters is only going to continue to increase in future years.

So, it's a smart idea to set your family up for success by creating a dedicated home office space. Home offices are a storage challenge—most double as both the household paperwork center and a professional workspace, and are expected to house both sets of materials, filing systems, and minutiae in a streamlined and organized way. Many home office spaces can transform into craft or hobby areas as well. Organizing all these parts of your life in one room is no easy feat. But, armed with a plan and the right tools, you can create the kind of home office that will meet your family's specific needs and give you peace of mind knowing that all those important documents are easily accessible and each have a place.

Office Spaces

At their best, home offices provide a home away from home, where work itself becomes a retreat. Home offices can do more than simply provide space for traditionally defined work activities. A unique design can create an environment that makes going to work a pleasure.

A slatted wall system is perfect for storing office supplies within easy reach.

A well-planned home office or craft center has a dedicated spot for just about everything. A slat wall with hangers, baskets, and shelves is easy to customize to your needs.

Sliding doors separate this home office from other living areas when it's time to get to work.

Adjustable shelving adapts to your changing needs.

Though a dedicated office space is ideal, it's possible to situate an office area in a room designed for another purpose. Find a quiet spot, preferably away from other family members' activity or entertainment rooms.

Guest rooms are a good option if you'd like an office large enough to receive clients (plus, the bedroom closet is a storage bonus!). Or, find a narrow, unused corridor that could be converted into office space. Sometimes, just a little space is enough, as long as it is quiet and well-organized.

Narrow bookshelves along a large wall can be all you need to fulfill all your office storage needs. These 10-inch-deep shelves provide ample storage space and complement the office's open layout perfectly.

An effective home office needn't be large. Plan space for a standard-size work surface—20 inches deep with an 18-inch clearance on each side of a computer—a comfortable chair, and plenty of drawers and cabinets.

Keeping your home office organized and uncluttered can make you more productive and keep you from getting stressed out. Make sure you store the things you work with most where you can easily reach them. Built-to-fit (BTF) bookcases on short and sloped walls can be functional and aesthetically appealing.

If there are high spaces you need to access regularly, consider including a library ladder in the design.

When it comes to office storage, think vertically. File cabinets form the base of every working surface, and built-in floor-to-ceiling bookcases utilize every square inch of the end wall.

Custom features help make the most of this unique attic space. The built-in work stations line opposing walls to maximize space, with plenty of cabinet storage and a divider unit that follows the ceiling slope. In addition, the large windows bring natural light into the space.

Suspended shelving can be installed anywhere and is a great solution for tight spaces.

Closets are prime real estate in any home, but if you can manage to clear one out, you can create a private, efficient office space that's instantly hidden behind closed doors.

If your office lacks cabinets and other closed storage but you have ample shelving, use bins and boxes to keep your workspace organized.

Antique boxes,

suitcases, or boxes made from

natural materials can be great display items themselves.

They're also great places to stash papers or office supplies.

Aluminum utility trays,

like those used in hotels, can hold paper

clips, writing utensils, scratch paper, or other office necessities.

Tip

Looking for creative or clever accessory storage items? Just take a look around your house. With a fresh eye, reconsider the array of boxes, baskets, buckets, bins, bowls, vases, old suitcases, jars, cups, carts, chests, cans, tins, trays… that is, everything that you already have. See if you can't find them a new home.

Woven steel baskets
designed for gym and pool lockers are
great for CDs, labels, ink cartridges,
and other items you use less frequently
but like to keep track of.

A large corner cabinet can be transformed into desk space and shelving space. The lower doors on the cabinet open to provide extra storage.

A closet or an alcove with wide doors keeps your home office within reach when you need it and hidden when you don't. A desk with slide-out compartments and an extendable keyboard tray help add depth to your closet office nook.

The goal for any home office is to create an efficient, compact work area where everything you need is within reach. By utilizing every nook and cranny to its fullest potential, even a room with minimal floor space can be transformed into a fully equipped office with ample elbowroom.

Built-in storage and floor-to-ceiling bookshelves keep everything neatly put away and right at your fingertips. A TV screen tucked into a corner built-in provides entertainment or access to news and financials with a spin of the task chair. And with the monitor and wires tucked under the desk hutch with a pullout drawer for the keyboard, this office manages to achieve a fairly clean, minimalist look.

Build a Bookcase

An attractive, substantial bookcase can cost $200, but you can build your own bookcase for a fraction of the cost in under an hour. To form the bookcase frame, arrange two 1 x 10 x 72" and two 1 x 10 x 36" planks on the floor and fasten with finish nails or thin wood screws.

Then cut four 1 x 10" shelves to length, place at the desired heights, and drive finish nails through the frame into the edge of each shelf. Allow a larger shelf space at the bottom for oversized books, and leave an opening at the foot of the bookcase to keep dust from accumulating.

To keep books from falling through the back of the bookcase, nail 1 x 4s (see p.216) horizontally across the back of each shelf space. For diagonal support, run picture-

hanging wire from screws placed at each of the four corners on the back of the unit to a fifth screw placed in the middle of the back of the unit. Pull the wire taut, making sure the unit remains level and square.

Good lighting is extremely important in an office, and a nice view is refreshing while working. For these reasons, home offices are usually located upstairs. However, with a little creativity, a basement room can be made into a comfortable and bright home office as well.

Papers and files are organized in bins for neat access.

A rolling filing cabinet keeps files in a convenient location that can be quickly tucked away.

Who says a basement has to be dark? A stationary window flanked by two spacious egress windows were carved out of the foundation wall, and a generously deep window well keeps natural light streaming inside.

Multiple workstations make optimum use of the available space in this converted basement. A computer station on one wall, an architect's drafting table opposite it, and a beautiful red oak filing cabinet in between them create a highly functional U-shaped desk arrangement.

All of this homeowner's sewing supplies are kept in one place and easily accessible.

While cubicles, metal file cabinets, and fluorescent lights may be appropriate (or merely functional) for the on-site office, few want to replicate that aesthetic in their own homes. At the same time, one has to foot the bill for home office equipment and storage, so it needs to be affordable as well as functional and attractive.

While this home office doubles as a linen closet and sewing center, there is still plenty of workspace and storage possibilities.

By locating the sewing center right next to the oversized linen closet, there's plenty of room for fabric samples and patterns.

Rolling file cabinets can be tucked out of the way when office work is complete.

A magnet board is a great place to store reminders and phone numbers without adding clutter to your work surface.

Even if you don't have a lot of room for an office, the right storage can create a functional workspace in a tight corner.

A compact row of lightweight drawers mounted to the wall keeps the bills, receipts, and mail in their own neat compartments rather than spread through the house.

This cabinet is large enough to hold binders and bins for larger documents, and the backlighting helps you find them when needed.

The space underneath your staircase may be just the right size for an office nook. Desks with drawers, tall shelving, and file cabinets can be arranged to fit neatly in that spot.

If your rolls of gift-wrapping paper are resting under ice skates in a closet, stuffed into the back of your laundry room, or bumping up behind the mason jars in your pantry, consider installing a gift-wrap center anywhere you have extra space. A few sturdy dowels mounted horizontally will hold all your rolls of gift wrap and ribbons, keeping them neat and accessible when you need them.

Creative Spaces

Creative spaces don't have to be messy or cluttered. By organizing your studio or workspace well, you might even open up space in your mind for new ideas. And, with a clutter-free hobby area all set up and waiting for you, you'll have more time to spend doing what you love, regardless of which hobby fills your free time.

Simple plank shelving can be affordable and elegant at the same time. With the aid of a simple desk, the shelving helps designate the alcove as a workspace without closing off the display from the rest of the home.

A wall of shelving with movable shelves and a variety of spacing can help you keep almost anything organized neatly and efficiently.

Baskets on simple, low shelving are excellent organizers. They can be removed for quick cleanup and replaced easily. The upper shelf can serve as a bench, table, or display shelf.

Most hobbies require space to spread out, and many people that enjoy the arts don't necessarily require their own studio. A dedicated room, however, is nice. Whether you are employed as an artist, musician, or crafter—or simply enjoy spending your leisure time dabbling in the arts—chances are you wish you had more space. Perhaps, however, you have more space than you know! By better organizing and storing your hobby-related items, you can free up substantial space to create.

Media storage all around this open space, along with plenty of electrical power and soundproofing, transform it into a home recording studio.

Spools of thread mounted on the wall stay organized and accessible.

Sewing and quilting are activities that require space to spread out, as well as a lot of storage for the various supplies. Good lighting, large surfaces for cutting fabric, and a comfortable place to sit are prerequisites for any good sewing room. Full-spectrum overhead lighting illuminates the details, making it easier to locate seams and match up intricate fabric designs.

Attics & Basements

Historically, attics and basements have been purely pragmatic spaces that are included in the home purely as part of its design given the local climate. Using these spaces for storage or extra living space is a fairly modern home development, and most people's attic and basement are both dramatically underutilized. Many are just empty boxes or cluttered, disorganized store rooms.

The most efficiently used basements and attics today are a combination of living space and overflow storage. As you think about how to best use your attic or basement, consider both your family's needs and the built-in sensibilities of your home. Build in plenty of space for storing less-frequently used items while you adapt these rooms to be suitable places to hang out, exercise, or play.

With solid forethought, any attic or basement can be adapted or reconfigured to fit the everyday living patterns of your family. By incorporating these extra spaces into your daily life along with some clever storage tricks, you'll be amazed at the usable space already available in your own home.

Living Areas

Finishing a basement or attic as an additional living space is a large project, and can be expensive. However, a finished basement or attic can sometimes more than double the usable living space in your home. Finished basement and attic spaces are also often safer storage spaces for valuables than unfinished basements or attics; the process of finishing the space inherently protects storage items from damage caused by moisture or insects. Remodeling your basement or attic might add just the extra space your home needs as your family grows.

Adjustable shelving allows you to store objects of multiple sizes, and to adapt the system to meet your needs.

Modular shelving along the long basement wall is a great use of space. This immense amount of shelving can house entire libraries of books, music, or other collectibles safely.

Interrupt long spans of shelving with open spaces to showcase artwork or other objects.

Enclosing ductwork is crucial to transforming the basement into living space.

Many people view attics and basements as out-of-the-way square footage and let them become overrun with fields of clutter and unidentified debris. Basements and attics, however, are already primed to be well integrated with the rest of the house as genuinely organized storage space.

In the case of basements, if you think of the space as an integral part of your home and treat it as you would any space on the main living levels, you will automatically use the area more efficiently. On the other hand, finished attics, with their strange combinations of sloping walls and ceilings, are hard enough to move around in comfortably, let alone to find places to store things. The upper wall space is suddenly gone, lost to the roof pitch as the ceiling crowds in. This means that you need to look toward the unusual and unique spaces that are created and utilize them to the best of your abilities.

With a little work, these spaces can be as neatly organized as the rest of your house.

To finish an attic space with a gable roof, knee walls have to be built at the sloping walls, and a knee wall is the perfect candidate for built-in storage. In this attic guest room, the extra tall ceilings allow for an open bookshelf in addition to enclosed cabinets for linen and bedding storage.

This bed nook places a child's sleeping space up against the sloped wall, where very little vertical space is needed.

A well-designed finished basement can offer many unique storage opportunities.

Ledges created by the dropped ceiling provide additional storage and display space.

A storage bench doubles as window seating and is conveniently located near a reading library, the stereo, and music collection.

A mini-office station with a calendar reminds you of your responsibilities for the day while offering immediate access to paper and pen, a phone, intercom, and baby monitor.

A flush, built-in cabinet so subtle you hardly know that it's there holds phone books, office supplies, or a small wastepaper basket.

This open attic utilizes available storage space without overwhelming the room. Small spaces like attics are easily crowded, so keep storage in finished attics along or within the walls.

Bookcases can serve as protective stair railings.

A humble home office can be organized under the slope of the gable ceiling at the top of the stairs of many attics. A simple 3 × 5-foot rug not only saves your floor from the wear and tear caused by a rolling office chair, but it helps to define the limits of the office area.

A basement bar is the perfect addition to a finished basement lounge area. The bar structure is self-contained, will not typically place additional storage demands on your space, and creates a focal point, both decoratively and functionally.

Built-in cabinets with glass doors are a great way to showcase dishware or spirits.

The space beneath the bar is perfect for extra cabinets or a mini-refrigerator.

In this narrow basement, the bar is placed in the center of the room rather than at the end or off to the side. This not only breaks up the space, but conceals exercise and storage areas behind the bar. The rounded wall on the left, which hides mechanicals as well as a bathroom and guest bedroom, softly pinches the long narrow room into two distinct sections.

Built-in shelving doubles, here, as a design feature, grounding the wallpaper's pattern to the rest of the room.

Additional bedrooms are a great use of finished attic space. This homeowner built a closet and shelving into the gable wall, which frees up the rest of the space for seating and sleeping. The white trim of the storage areas helps to balance out the bright print of the wallpaper.

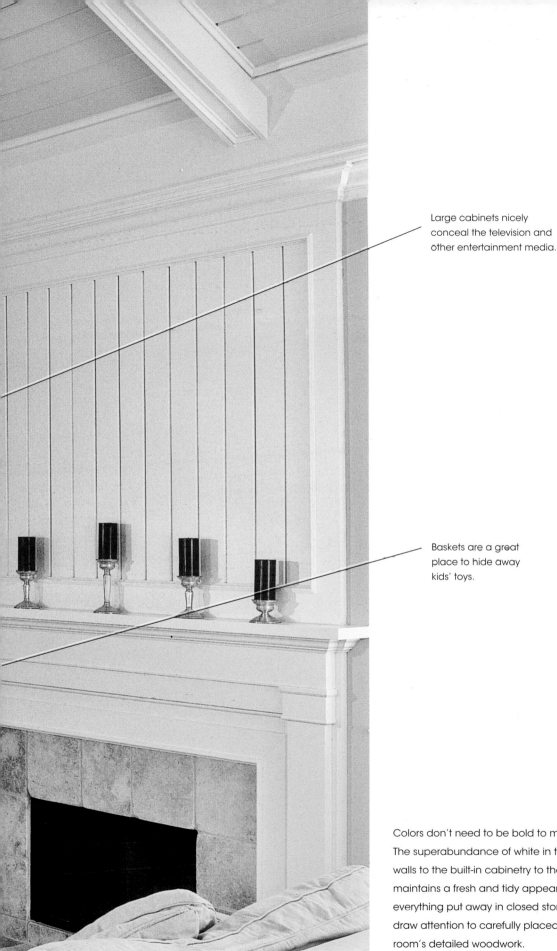

Large cabinets nicely conceal the television and other entertainment media.

Baskets are a great place to hide away kids' toys.

Colors don't need to be bold to make a strong impression. The superabundance of white in this room—from the walls to the built-in cabinetry to the ceiling to the sofas—maintains a fresh and tidy appearance. And with most everything put away in closed storage, the white surfaces draw attention to carefully placed display items and the room's detailed woodwork.

Playrooms

While designated playrooms are every child's dream, they can be a parent's delight as well. Converting a basement or attic into a child's play space can keep the noise, clutter, and mayhem of play safely apart from the rest of the home.

Built-in kneewalls are the perfect opportunity for additional storage of toys or homework supplies.

Playrooms can be adapted easily into shared spaces so that caregivers can get some work done while keeping an eye on the children. Placing a computer workstation against an attic kneewall can create more play space in the center of the room and provide a spot for the children's own projects or homework.

A few nice built-in cabinets provide perfect toy storage in a child's playroom. And with a matching custom wood cover over electric baseboard radiators, the otherwise hot mechanical is safe for children to play around or on.

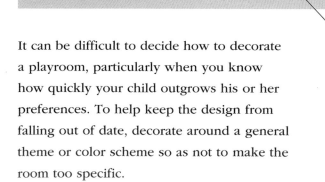

It can be difficult to decide how to decorate a playroom, particularly when you know how quickly your child outgrows his or her preferences. To help keep the design from falling out of date, decorate around a general theme or color scheme so as not to make the room too specific.

Movable toy bins are a great option for quick clean-up.

Store children's books on low shelves that are accessible to little hands.

Transform a Hall into a Chalkboard

For whatever reason, children love writing on walls. Which is a problem unless they write on a surface meant to be written upon. Chalkboard paint provides just that surface. And you can make your own chalkboard paint by mixing:

3 teaspoons acrylic paint [color of choice]
1½ teaspoons glazing medium [water-based]
½ teaspoon powder tile grout

Apply two to three coats of paint with a regular paintbrush. Between each coat, sand the dried surface with a 400-grit or higher sandpaper, then wipe away the dust.

Once the last coat is dry, you need to condition your new chalkboard. Place a piece of chalk on its side and rub over the entire surface. Wipe clean with a felt cloth, and then again with a slightly damp cloth. For a finished appearance, frame the painted area with door casing.

This child's playroom also serves as their workspace. The room is designed to be comfortable, organized, and fun so that work can be incorporated into a world of play. A good way to tie together a room that has multiple uses is to repeat each of the room's main fabrics, colors, and prints in at least three different places.

Houses are built proportionate to adult bodies, which can often leave little ones feeling disadvantaged. Inevitably, their favorite play spaces are the cozy nooks and crannies that allow them to feel completely in charge of their own environment.

An artist's painting on canvas covers a play space under the stairs. Inside the ship's galley (inset), we find a clever play space, which is also accessible from the adjoining closet.

Parents agree that toy clutter is a real problem in any room of the house, especially in the playroom. Adequate storage space in the playroom can keep the rest of your home from looking like the fallout from a toy explosion. If kids are required to put everything away before taking a nap or leaving the play area for another activity, they will grow accustomed to looking for things in their place and putting them back where they belong.

This colorful basement incorporates shelves and cabinets along the entire length of a wall to create an interesting backdrop for the play space, as well as plenty of storage.

Colors are vibrant, but not too childlike, so the space can grow along with the children. Hard-to-reach items are easily accessible by smaller kids by using the sturdy, built-in bench. Bins slide out for storing extra-deep items.

Exercise Rooms

If you are disciplined when it comes to fitness, all you need is a resistance band, jump rope, or yoga ball for stretching and strength training. But let's face it: most of us require some kind of motivation to get in shape. The first step to treating our bodies well is to have a dedicated fitness space.

Important things to keep in mind when adding an exercise room to your home include good lighting, adequate ventilation, and bright, cheery colors to keep you moving. And don't forget ample towel storage!

Low shelving is the perfect storage solution for an attic exercise room.

Adequate ventilation and cooling in an attic exercise room is a must. There should be at least two operable windows so you can create a cross-breeze in the space. Check with your builder to determine if your attic floor joists can support the weight of heavy machinery.

A variety of exercise equipment in a dedicated space can help you
remain focused and inspired in your workout regimen. The full-wall mirrors
create the sense of more space and allow you to check on your form
while exercising.

Unfinished Storage Areas

The main considerations for basic storage in an unfinished basement are how to keep items organized and accessible and how to protect them from inhospitable conditions such as flooding, condensation, and damp concrete surfaces. Often, creative, durable shelving is the answer.

Custom shelving in an unfinished basement can be strictly utilitarian or it can have a more finished look. This practical shelf is anchored to the ceiling joists above, creating more room on the top shelf.

Items in plastic tubs or other sealed containers can be stored on the floor.

Basement stairs offer multiple options for creative and out-of-the-way storage.

Shelves along an open stairwell wall can accommodate loads of smaller items and can double as backup pantry storage.

Utility shelves are easy and inexpensive to make and take up much less space than piles of boxes. They also make it easy to find what you're looking for without shuffling around all those other boxes to get at it.

Freestanding utility shelving can be built or bought cheaply and assembled quickly.

Shelving can easily be added between the joists of an unfinished attic or basement ceiling.

Small shelving units mounted to the underside of your steps are an inexpensive complement to your other storage plans for the nook beneath the basement stairs.

Build Your Own Shelving

Unfinished attics are often goldmines of underutilized storage. The structure is usually completely exposed; with no plaster or drywall, there's no longer any problem finding a place to anchor a shelf, ceiling hook, or closet rod.

Build Shelves Around a Gable Window

Building shelving around a gable window is easy, inexpensive, and a terrific use of space. The sloped ceiling of a gable roof makes any store-bought shelving either impossible to use or an inefficient use of space.

Cut pairs of 2 × 4 shelving braces to size that span from floor to ceiling, then fasten together with 14½" cleats at each shelf location. Fasten the braces to the rafters and at the floor. Cut shelves to size from ½" plywood, then nail in place to the cleats.

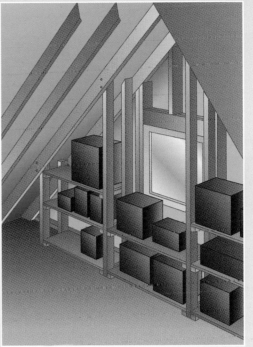

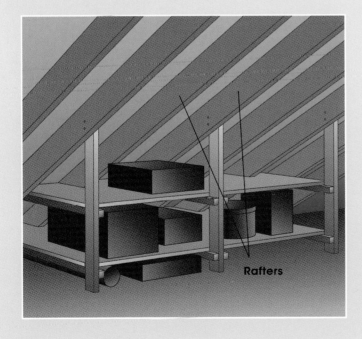

Rafters

Build Shelves Between Rafters

The space between rafters is difficult to work with because the angle of the roof makes it tough to retrieve items pushed to the back and prevents boxes from being stacked very high.

To build your own shelving for this space, nail a pair of ledgers to the rafters, one on each side, then attach the front of the shelves to studs spanning from the rafters to floor. Notch plywood or particle-board shelves to fit around the rafters.

Temperatures in an unfinished attic can fluctuate drastically; take care not to store items that could spoil or warp in extreme heat or cold.

Unused furniture that is light and bulky is a good candidate for storage in the attic.

Unfinished attic space can be a great location for long-term storage, especially for bulky, lightweight items like boxes of holiday decorations. A storage deck made of plastic decking panels makes it possible to use most of the storage space in your unfinished attic.

A retractable ladder makes accessing your unfinished attic quick and easy. Purchase one in a kit, or build it yourself.

If installing a walkway, take care not to compress insulation, which will decrease its effectiveness.

To access items in the attic, you can create a walkway with plastic panels staggered in steppingstone fashion. Include at least one panel per joist space and install additional panels, as necessary.

Garages

Not long ago, the garage was considered optional in modern home design. According to garage industry figures, in 1950 only 47 percent of new homes were built with garages.

Today, 87 percent of new homes include garages, which now are expected to hold a lot more than cars. For many people, the garage also offers easy access to yard and garden necessities, warehouses building tools and materials, and acts as a foster home for all of the orphaned stuff that wasn't wanted inside the house. Plus, the garage is expected to serve as the craftsman's workshop and the mechanic's workspace.

Believe it or not, even a modestly sized garage can handle all these duties and more, but the only way to get there is to have the right storage plan.

As evidenced by recent spikes in sales of garage storage products, remodeling the garage is a new trend for homeowners who want a dream space that is neat and orderly, with plenty of room to stock their latest tools and toys.

Multi-purpose Garage

Every family is different and, therefore, uses their garage storage differently. Regardless of what type of items you are hoping to store, an organized system is essential.

Ideally, about one-third of your garage should be used for storage. Cabinets are the most immediate, easiest solution—however, there are many creative storage solutions for garages, many of which will be explored on the next few pages.

Constructed from high and medium density fiberboard, this system of matching wall-mounted cabinetry and floor units is a great option if an uncluttered, uniform workspace is important to you.

Adjustable feet compensate for an uneven floor to keep storage cabinets level.

Locking cabinets protect possessions and people, especially children. Power tools, poisonous or toxic chemicals, and combustible materials should be stored in locked cabinets.

Rolling bases can be stored at the perimeter and pulled into a convenient working arrangement when a project is underway.

A well-organized, well-planned garage offers space for many activities. This oversized, three-car garage serves as a play space for children, a workshop for adults, and a storage space for hobby and seasonal items.

An extra refrigerator is the perfect place for sodas, holiday overflow, or everyday backup food storage.

Heavy-duty shelves hold seasonal items such as a snowblower, sleds, and cushions for the lawn furniture.

Use a slatted wall storage system to keep everything organized, from sports equipment to ladders and lawn tools.

Take advantage of otherwise-wasted space: Tuck racks above the overhead garage door tracks. These shelves hold about 250 pounds each.

Mount a Library Ladder

Upper walls and ceilings are ideal spaces for shelves and storage bins, but pulling out a ladder to get to your stuff can literally be a drag.

Instead, mount a library ladder to the front of the shelves. The ladder hangs at the edge of the shelves, well out of the way until you need to use it. Then, roll the ladder into place, and you have safe access to even the highest shelves.

A plywood floor and lightweight shelving converted this garage attic to ideal storage space, reserving precious floor space in the garage for other purposes. One caveat—store only items that can safely endure temperature extremes. Garage attics can experience swings of more than 100° F from summer to winter in some climates.

Hooks mounted on the wall are the perfect
place to keep large sports equipment.

Pegboard offers an almost infinite number
of places to hang tools and toys.

Organization is the key to using one space for a variety of activities. The space in this garage is loosely divided into activity centers—a household workshop, a car and motorcycle maintenance workshop, and a gardening center. Because the area is also used as a play space for young children, tall cabinets are especially important—they provide space to keep hazardous materials and power tools out of reach.

Garage drawers can be fitted with organizers to make small parts easy to find.

Shop Storage

Almost all garage-organizing projects have the same goal in mind: to free up floor space in the middle of the garage to park.

To this end, line the walls of the garage with a material you can use to hang tools and equipment anywhere you like, whether it's plywood, slat-board, or a specially designed organizing system.

Then add some cabinets. Kitchen cabinetry is as useful in the garage as it is in the kitchen. If you can't afford new cabinets, recycle the old cabinets from your kitchen when you do a remodel or pick up some inexpensive reclaimed cabinets at a salvage center.

A well-organized garage tends to look like a centrifuge that has just finished spinning—its contents are clearly separated and organized by type around the perimeter.

The garage shown here utilizes a comprehensive system including a slat wall structure, storage cabinets, lockers, and shelves, all with a rugged, stainless steel finish. The matching cabinets and appliances pleasantly trick the eye into thinking that the garage is a mostly open and empty space. In fact, a quick inventory reveals that this garage is able to neatly allow for more storage than many garages twice its size.

Casters on all of the base cabinets and appliances make it easy to rearrange the garage when necessary, or to wheel some gear closer to where you're working.

The slogan of progress is changing from the full dinner pail to the full garage.

—Herbert Hoover

Heavy-duty pull-out drawers on this workshop base cabinet help keep tools organized.

Deep, tall base cabinets are perfect for bulky items like shopvacs and garden hoses, or extra chains, rope, and bungee cords.

A refrigerator/freezer offers overflow storage to families who buy supplies in bulk or who just need extra space around the holidays.

Locks on cabinets keep dangerous equipment out of the hands of children and offer another level of protection against theft.

The display panels traditionally used to organize merchandise for retailers inspired the garage system pictured here. That might seem strange at first, but if you think about it, the principles of good merchandising are also the foundation of a well-designed garage. In both cases the system needs to be lightweight, easy to install, and durable, as well as versatile enough to be configured for unique needs.

Accessories tailored to store specific items are more likely to get used than generic hooks.

Insider Advice: Tricks from the Pros

Athenée Mastrangelo, Professional Organizer
Action: Chaos, Orlando, FL

- Use a rolling storage cabinet for storing your tools or sporting goods. Roll it out to wherever you need it and when you're done, just roll it back to its place.
- To keep your garden tools clean and free from rusting, store them in a bucket with sand. Hose your tools off when you are done and store them back in the bucket of sand. Before every use, spray them with a non-stick spray to keep the dirt from sticking.
- When storing paint, put a dash of the paint on the outside of the can to easily identify the color without having to open the can. Before sealing the can, cover the opening with plastic wrap for air tightness, then securely cover the can with the lid and store it upside down to avoid getting a dry film over your paint.

Frequently used chemicals and tools are kept in an easy-to-reach area.

Most of the components of this well-organized garage are modular and adjustable. Notice the wide variety of storage solutions: hooks, shelves, drawers, containers, cabinets with sliding doors, and a combination of closed and open containers.

A relatively small garage corner can pack in a lot of storage by using the right cabinetry.

A good workbench is headquarters for home projects, whether for a tinkerer, hobbyist, or professional craftsman. It provides a central location for the tools one uses most and a workspace at which to use them.

Your work area should have plenty of storage without crowding you. Designing your workbench with enough shelves, drawers, compartments, and hooks will help keep everything you need at your fingertips. There are many accessories designed to keep workbenches clear of clutter without having to invest in a complete garage system. If your space is significantly limited, consider a folding workbench that can fall flat against the wall when not in use.

If you can dedicate an entire garage wall to your workspace, do it. People tend to collect tools and materials over time and it's convenient to put everything in one place.

Pegboard backing is a convenient way to hang tools in an easy-to-reach place.

Have a fire extinguisher on hand if you store flammable solvents, or do any soldering or welding.

Whatever activity you engage in, whether gardening, painting, metalwork, or auto repair, rolling toolboxes are a great way to keep together all the tools and supplies you need for your project. Shallow drawers near the top allow room for lightweight tools, while heavier items can be stored in the cabinet below.

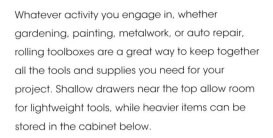

Tip

Stray bolts driving you nuts? An easy and inexpensive way to organize nuts, bolts, and other stray hardware is to sort them into glass or plastic jars and secure the lids to the bottom of a shelf. Because you can see everything you have, it'll be easier to find exactly what you're after.

Another way to squeeze more storage space into a small work area is to install deep pull-out shelves. Your tools and supplies will be kept in order within a minimum amount of wall space.

Utility Systems

The key to making room for all of your tools and materials is to start at the walls and build up, not out. Garage ceilings are typically quite high, often eight or nine feet, so there is a lot of ceiling and upper wall space that can be utilized for storage. With the help of sturdy, easily accessible ceiling suspension storage and tall wall shelving, you can make room for everything.

This rolling cart holds brooms, hoes, shovels, and other long tools.

With this innovative shelving system, a sturdy bracket strip displaces weight across the entire length of a garage wall. Bracket tracks for shelves or hooks are then suspended down the wall from the strips for easily adjustable storage.

A mix of freestanding shelves, open and closed cabinets, and track shelving make it possible for you to store everything you need and find whatever you're looking for—even from across the room.

Removable shelves for lightweight use are easily suspended from eye hooks drilled into the wood trusses in the ceiling.

Need shelving in your garage? There are a number of systems available:

Track and bracket: Tracks are secured to a wall stud, and the snap-in brackets make it easy to adjust shelf heights.

Track and clip: Two sets of tracks are installed on opposing surfaces, and a shelf rests on four clips, one at each corner.

Shelf bracket/L-brace: The shelf surface is secured directly to the bracket, making it sturdier than most track and bracket systems. Since the bracket is attached to the wall directly, however, it is not as easy to adjust the shelf height.

Z-brace: Directly attaches to the wall and to the shelf like the L-brace, but the diagonal bracing provides additional shelf strength.

Stud bracket: A heavy-duty bracket that wraps around an exposed stud.

Ledger boards: Horizontal strips, usually 2 × 4s or 1 × 3s, that support shelving on three sides.

Sturdy, adjustable shelves are easy to install and offer a convenient place to safely store those larger, lightweight items off the floor. The brackets attach to the hangers and rest against the wall. The weight of the shelving holds the brackets in place—no screws required.

Gardening & Lawn Care

The 22 billion dollar U.S. lawn and garden market proves we are a proud and picky nation when it comes to the greenery immediately surrounding our homes. It's almost impossible to own a home without a slow creep of lawn/garden care equipment and products gathering valuable space over time. Before investing further space (and dollars) in a stand-alone shed, assess your garage walls. Can you turn this space into vertical storage?

In sight and within reach: The two key words in lawn and garden storage are visibility and accessibility. Grid storage systems are particularly appropriate for lawn and garden tools.

A dedicated storage cabinet helps keep potting tools and small planters organized and off the floor. Look for heavy-duty cabinetry that can stand some wear and tear.

Insider Advice: Tricks from the Pros

Karen Law, Design/Professional Organization
Contained Design, Minneapolis, MN

• Divide the garage into zones that fit your work and lifestyle. (Don't set aside a wood shop area if you don't like working with wood, for example.)
• If it's broken, send it to the repair shop or throw it out!
• Have a garage sale and make some money on the items no longer needed.
• Organize the remaining items. Hang it, hook it, get it off the floor.
• Donate items you no longer use. Many charities will pick up donated items. Some communities have Internet bulletin boards where people trade unwanted items.
• Involve the whole family. In most families, every member is part of the problem, and everyone needs to be part of the solution.
• Containerize. Use bins, stackable totes, and containers as much as possible.
• Label every container with a list of its contents.
• Put all poisons and hazardous items in locking cabinets and keep them locked.
• Add plenty of light. You can't use what you can't find.

Tool Storage

Effective tool storage requires careful management: dedicate boxes and drawers for small loose tools, drill bits, small hand tools, nuts and bolts, nails, switches, and any other small bits and pieces you accumulate. Unless you have an extraordinary visual memory, label the drawers. It will save you from having to open each and every drawer or box to figure out where you put something. If you can, mount tool cabinets on casters; they'll be easy to move around the garage.

Keep clamps off the floor. You can use cement anchors to attach 2 x 4s to the wall for clamp storage.

For a modestly sized tool chest, you could spend anywhere from 50 to 500 dollars, depending on the brand. In most cases you get what you pay for. If you get the cheapest box you can find, it will likely rust or break down within a relatively short time. Spending too much may buy you features you never use. Figure out the size and features you really need, then judge the product by the quality of construction details.

Look for a design with a safety feature that prevents drawers from opening if the unit is accidentally tilted or tipped.

Line drawers to keep tools from slipping around and to prevent rust. You can find inexpensive 1/16" polyethylene drawer liners that come in 48 × 25" sheets.

Look for a flip top with a lock on it.

Full-width drawer pulls are a convenient feature for tool drawers.

Graduated drawer depth helps keep small items from getting buried.

Make sure your tool drawers open with ball bearing slides.

The inside of the box as well as the outside should be coated with a baked enamel finish or another corrosion-resistant finish.

Some storage items make contradictory demands—they need to be right at your fingertips and out of the way. Wall hooks, clips, and forks are the perfect solution to both. There are many options today that are so versatile they can look as though they were tailor-made to fit your belongings.

Garden tool organizers mount to the wall studs to keep shovels, rakes, and other hand tools easily accessible yet out of the way.

A few hooks and bracketed baskets make an easy storage section for painters' materials. The thermoplastic walls are easy to clean and won't scratch, ding, dent, or rust—important considerations when storing messy chemicals, paints, and tools.

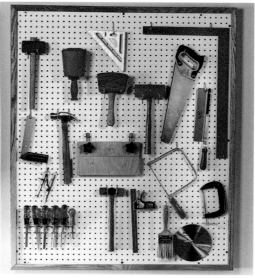

Pegboard systems are versatile and can accommodate many different kinds of items, from hand tools to saw blades and small nuts and bolts.

There's no reason to track outdoor toys and athletic equipment back and forth through the house. Designate space for them in the garage. Footballs, snowboards, basketballs, tennis racquets, soccer balls, and golf clubs can all fit on racks and in storage bins in the garage much more easily than they can be jammed into coat closets inside the house. Whether you find that the perfect system to store your goods is as simple as a hook or a bucket, or a more complex system with brackets, pulleys, and cantilevers, every space and storage problem has a solution.

A bike rack consisting of a single expandable post, held between the floor and ceiling by pressure is a trouble-free way to get a few bikes in order. Other bike storage systems include hanging hooks for walls and ceilings, bracketless racks, wall-leaning styles, and even hoist-and-pulley systems that do the heavy lifting for you.

Upper cabinets in the garage placed about 48" from the floor, at about the same height as those in your kitchen, leave just enough space below to hang a bicycle—which also happens to be plenty of room for a golf bag, tennis racquet, or anything else that is too big to be stored behind closed doors.

These panels come in two sizes: 4-ft. × 15" or 8-ft. × 15". They stack one above the other, with the seam completely hidden under a slot. The cost is approximately $170 per 30 square feet of paneling. You can cut the panels with a regular wood saw, so they're easy to customize. There is a large assortment of different hooks and accessories that you can buy separately.

Use creative fixtures along with a slatted wall or pegboard system to make the most of your wall space and protect your tools. In addition to hooks and hangers, magnetic bar strips and shelving can be used to keep frequently used or heavy items safe along the walls of your garage space.

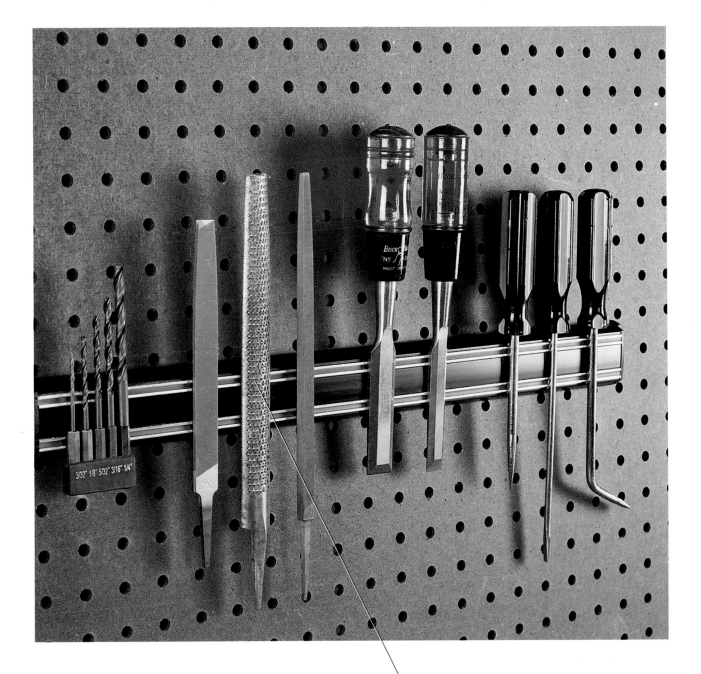

Store chisels, files, awls, and other metal tools on magnetic bar strips.

In garages outfitted for restoration, workbenches are generally about two feet wide, four to six feet long, 30 to 40 inches high, and durable. Beyond that, there's plenty of room for creativity. This workbench was made out of salvaged lumber from a bowling alley. The cabinet it rests on was salvaged from the woman's glove department of a defunct retail store.

This roll-away toolbox stores flush against a wall. The bottom portion is on casters so it can be rolled over to the project. The more organized a person is, the more he or she appreciates the ability to compartmentalize tools according to type and size.

Tip

There are many terrific shelf, drawer, and display units on the market, some built especially for garage storage. While many of them are wonderfully designed and efficient, they also can be quite expensive.

Before investing in those units, check out local salvage stores, re-use centers, and other second-hand stores. Many communities also have online bulletin boards where such items are shared and traded, most often at no charge. You may find unusual solutions for your storage needs.

These drawers are lined with a soft, absorbent cork. The cork keeps the tools from sliding around and helps to prevent rust by absorbing excess water that finds its way into the drawer. Some mechanics prefer rubber matting over cork to line their tool drawers.

Resource Guide

A listing of resources for information, designs, and products found in *Common Sense Storage*

Introduction

Page 4
Office storage by
Schulte
513-277-3700
www.schultestorage.com

Getting Organized

Page 6
Storage by
California Closets
1.888.336.9707
www.californiaclosets.com

Page 9 (top)
© Andrea Rugg (Top)

Page 9 (lower)
Storage by
Rubbermaid
888-895-2110
www.rubbermaid.com

Page 12
cabinets by
KraftMaid Cabinetry, Inc.
800-571-1990
www.kraftmaid.com

Page 13
Monica Friel
Professional Home & Office
Organizer, member NAPO
Chaos to Order
P.O. Box 316601
Chicago, IL 60631
847-825-8400
888-88-CHAOS
www.chaostoorder.com

Kitchens & Pantries

Resource Guide (continued)

Page 26 (bottom)
Pull-out kitchen storage by
Distinctions Cabinetry
800-203-0538
Distinctions Cabinetry is available
exclusively at Home Depot
www.distinctionscabinetry.com

Page 27 (top)
Pull-out kitchen storage by
SieMatic
888-316-2665
www.siematic.com

Page 27 (bottom, both)
Pull-out-kitchen storage by
Plain & Fancy Custom Cabinetry
800-447-9006
www.plainfancycabinets.com

Page 28
Kitchen cabinets by
Aristokraft
www.aristokraft.com

Page 29 (top)
Kitchen storage by
SieMatic
888-316-2665
www.siematic.com

Page 29 (Bottom)
© The Interior Archive / Andrew Wood

Page 30
© The Interior Archive / Fritz Von Der
Schulenburg

Page 31
© Brian Vanden Brink for Ted Wengren
Architect

Page 31
Audra Leonard
Professional Organizer, member NAPO
Artistic Organizing
P.O. Box 431
Anoka, MN 55303-0431
763-218-5298
www.ArtisticOrganizing.com

Page 32
Kitchen storage by
IKEA
800-434-4532
www.ikea.com

Page 33 (top)
© Brand X Pictures

Page 33 (bottom)
Kitchen cabinets by
Plain & Fancy Custom Cabinetry
800-447-9006
www.plainfancycabinets.com

Page 34 and 35 (bottom)
Pantry by
California Closets
800-274-6754
www.calclosets.com

Page 35 (top)
Pantry by
ClosetMaid
www.closetmaid.com

Page 36 (both)
Kitchen storage by
Plain & Fancy Custom Cabinetry
800-447-9006
www.plainfancycabinets.com

Page 38 (right)
© The Interior Archive / Fritz Von Der
Schulenburg

Page 39
© Andrea Rugg
Wine cellar by
Tea 2 Architects
612-929-2800
www.tea2architects.com

Bathrooms, Linens & Laundry

Resource Guide (continued)

Page 64
Media storage by
elfa® International and distributed by
elfa® North America
800-394-3532
www.elfa.com

Page 65
Bathroom cabinets by
Diamond Cabinets
www.diamondcabinets.com

Page 66
Laundry room furnishings by
IKEA
800-434-4532
www.ikea.com

Page 67 (top)
Cabinets by
Merillat Industries
www.merillat.com

Page 67 (bottom)
Laundry room design by
Plato Woodwork, Inc.
800-328-5924
www.platowoodwork.com

Page 68
Laundry room design by
California Closets
800-274-6754
www.calclosets.com

Page 69 (bottom)
Photo © Andrea Rugg
Laundry room design by
Robert Gerloff Residential Architects
Ltd.
Minneapolis, Minnesota
612-927-5913
www.ResidentialArchitects.com

Family & Entertainment Rooms

Resource Guide (continued)

Page 93
Storage and furnishings by
IKEA
800-434-4532
www.ikea.com

Page 94 (top)
Shelving by
Room and Board
800-486-6554
www.roomandboard.com

Page 94 (bottom)
Shelving by
California Closets
800-274-6754
www.calclosets.com

Page 95
© The Interior Archive / Fritz Von Der
Schulenburg

Page 96
Galvanized cube shelving by
The Container Store
888-CONTAIN
www.thecontainerstore.com

Page 97 (top)
© Brian Vanden Brink for Scholz and
Barclay Architects

Page 97 (lower)
© The Interior Archive / Tim Beddow

Page 99
© The Interior Archive / Tim Beddow

Page 100
© Brian Vanden Brink

Page 101 (top)
© Brand X Pictures

Page 101 (lower)
Photo Courtesy of Quigley Architects,
Mpls., MN

Page 102 and 103 (top)
© Brian Vanden Brink

Page 103 (lower)
© Brian Vanden Brink for Christina
Oliver Interior Design

Page 104
© Getdecorating.com

Page 105
Understairs storage by
elfa® International
and distributed by
elfa® North America
800-394-3532
www.elfa.com

Page 105
J. Colvin Consulting

Page 106
Storage and furnishings by
IKEA
800-434-4532
www.ikea.com

Page 107
Storage by
California Closets
800-274-6754
www.calclosets.com

Bedrooms

Page 110
Bedroom furnishings by
Room and Board
800-486-6554
www.roomandboard.com

Page 112
Closet system by
Space Storage Solutions
612-227-7340
www.spacestoragesolutions.com

Page 113
Closet system by
ClosetMaid
www.closetmaid.com

Page 114
Closet storage by
Distinctions Cabinetry
Distinctions Cabinetry is available
exclusively at Home Depot
800-203-0538
www.distinctionscabinetry.com

Page 115
Closet storage by
Plato Woodwork, Inc.
800-328-5924
www.platowoodwork.com

Page 116 (top)
© Getdecorating.com

Page 116
Suntunnel lighting by
VELUX-America, Inc.
800-88-VELUX
www.veluxUSA.com

Page 117
Closet system by
ClosetMaid
www.closetmaid.com

Page 118 (left)
California Closets
1.888.336.9707
www.californiaclosets.com

Page 118 (right)
Pull-out baskets by
ClosetMaid
www.closetmaid.com

Page 119 (top)
Closet by
Stacks and Stacks
866-376-6856
www.stacksandstacks.com

Page 119 (bottom)
Closet system by
The Container Store
888-CONTAIN
www.thecontainerstore.com

Resource Guide (continued)

Page 120
Closet system by
Distinctions Cabinetry
800-203-0538
Distinctions Cabinetry is available
exclusively at Home Depot
www.distinctionscabinetry.com

Page 121
Kasey Vejar, Professional Organizer,
member NAPO
Simply Organized, Inc.
P.O. Box 12652
Shawnee Mission, KS 66214
913-269-5920
www.kcorganizers.com

Page 122 (left)
Hanging storage by
The Company Store
800-323-8000
www.thecompanystore.com

**Page 122 (top and bottom) and
Page 123 (top)**
The Container Store
888-CONTAIN
www.thecontainerstore.com

Page 123 (right)
California Closets
1.888.336.9707
www.californiaclosets.com

Page 123 (bottom)
IKEA
800-434-4532
www.ikea.com

Page 124
Storage and furnishings by
IKEA
800-434-4532
www.ikea.com

Page 125 (both)
Closet storage manufactured by
elfa® International
and distributed by
elfa® North America
800-394-3532
www.elfa.com

Page 128
Storage system by
IKEA
800-434-4532
www.ikea.com

Page 129 (top)
Portable storage system by
Stacks and Stacks
866-376-6856
www.stacksandstacks.com

Page 129 (bottom)
Portable storage system by
The Company Store
800-323-8000
www.thecompanystore.com

Page 130 (lower)
© Brian Vanden Brink

Page 130 (top) and 131 (right)
Portable storage system by
Stacks and Stacks
866-376-6856
www.stacksandstacks.com

Page 131 (bottom)
Portable storage by
The Container Store
888-CONTAIN
www.thecontainerstore.com

Page 132 (bottom)
Photo © Andrea Rugg
Design by
David Heide Design Studio
Minneapolis, Minnesota
612-337-5060
www.dhdstudio.com

Page 133 (top)
Photo © Andrea Rugg
Built-in by
Mindy Sloo, Architect
Minneapolis, Minnesota
612-870-7098

Page 133 (bottom)
California Closets
1.888.336.9707
www.californiaclosets.com

Page 134 - 135 (all)
Photos © Andrea Rugg
Design by
LOCUS Architecture, Ltd.
612-706-5600
www.locusarchitecture.com

Page 136
Murphy bed by
Modern Spaces
415-357-9900
www.ModernSpaces.com

Page 137
Furnishings by
IKEA
800-434-4532
www.ikea.com

Page 138 (top)
Under bed storage by
Room and Board
800-486-6554
www.roomandboard.com

Page 138 (lower)
© Brian Vanden Brink for Julie Snow,
Architect

Page 141
Bed frame by
IKEA
800-434-4532
www.ikea.com

Page 142 (top)
Bedroom storage by
Distinctions Cabinetry
800-203-0538
Distinctions Cabinetry is available
exclusively at Home Depot
www.distinctionscabinetry.com

Page 142 (bottom)
Storage and furnishings by
IKEA
800-434-4532
www.ikea.com

Page 143
© Jessie Walker

Page 144
© Brian Vanden Brink for Sally Westin
Architects

Page 145
Cube storage by
The Company Store
800-323-8000
www.thecompanystore.com

Resource Guide (continued)

Home Offices

Page 146
Office furnishings by
California Closets
1.888.336.9707
www.californiaclosets.com

Page 149
Office furnishings by
California Closets
1.888.336.9707
www.californiaclosets.com

Page 150 and 151
© Brian Vanden Brink

Page 152 (top)
© Beateworks, Inc. / Alamy

Page 152 (lower)
© Karen Melvin

Page 154 (top)
Bamboo box storage by
The Container Store
888-CONTAIN
www.thecontainerstore.com

Page 154 (bottom, both)
Basket storage by
The Museum of Useful Things
800-515-2707
www.themut.com

Page 155 (top)
Home furnishings by
IKEA
800-434-4532
www.ikea.com

Page 155 (lower)
© The Interior Archive / Eduardo
Munoz

Page 156
Skylights by
VELUX-America, Inc.
800-88-VELUX
www.veluxUSA.com

Page 158
© Andrea Rugg for Newland
Architecture

Page 159
Office design by
Newland Architecture
Minneapolis, Minnesota
612-926-2424
www.newlandarchitecture.com

Page 160
Home office storage by
California Closets
1.888.336.9707
www.californiaclosets.com

Page 161
Home office storage by
Distinctions Cabinetry
800-203-0538
Distinctions Cabinetry is available
exclusively at Home Depot
www.dlstinctionscabinetry.com

Page 162
Home furnishings by
IKEA
800-434-4532
www.ikea.com

Page 163 (top)
Design by
Quigley Architects
Minneapolis, Minnesota
612-692-8850
www.quigleyarchitects.com

Page 163 (bottom)
Home storage by
California Closets
1.888.336.9707
www.californiaclosets.com

Page 164
© The Interior Archive / Andrew Wood

Page 165 (top)
Home storage by
California Closets
1.888.336.9707
www.californiaclosets.com

Page 165 (lower)
© The Interior Archive / Fritz Von Der
Schulenburg

Page 166
Home furnishings by
IKEA
800-434-4532
www.ikea.com

Page 167
Photo © Andrea Rugg
Sewing room design by
Awad & Koontz Architect Builders Inc.
Minneapolis, Minnesota
www.awadandkoontz.com

Attics & Basements

Page 168
© Andrea Rugg for Locus
Architecture,
Cabinets by Thompson Woodworks
and Mfg. Co.

Page 171
© Anne Gummerson /
www.AnneGummersonPhoto.com

Page 172
© David Livingston /
www.davidduncanlivingston.com

Page 173 (top)
© Brian Vanden Brink

Page 174 (bottom)
© Jeff Kruger

Page 174
Photo © Andrea Rugg
Attic design by
Tea 2 Architects
612-929-2800
www.tea2architects.com

Page 175
Photo © Andrea Rugg
Attic design by
Robert Gerloff Residential Architecture
Minneapolis, Minnesota
612-927-5913
www.ResidentialArchitects.com

Page 176
Photo © Andrea Rugg
Basement bar by
Newland Architecture
Minneapolis, Minnesota
612-926-2424
www.newlandarchitecture.com

Page 177
Attic storage by
California Closets
1.888.336.9707
www.californiaclosets.com

Page 178
© David Livingston /
www.davidduncanlivingston.com

Page 180
© David Livingston /
www.davidduncanlivingston.com

Page 181
Photo © Andrea Rugg
Basement playroom design by
LOCUS Architecture, Ltd.
612-706-5600
www.locusarchitecture.com

Page 182
Attic skylights by
VELUX-America, Inc.
800-88-VELUX
www.veluxUSA.com

Page 184 (both)
Photo © Andrea Rugg
Basement hideaway design by
LOCUS Architecture, Ltd.
612-706-5600
www.locusarchitecture.com
Canvas art by
Kyle Fredrickson
612-747-0635

Page 185
Photo © Andrea Rugg
Basement design by
Robert Gerloff Residential Architecture
Minneapolis, Minnesota
612-927-5913
www.ResidentialArchitects.com

Page 186
Attic skylights by
VELUX-America, Inc.
800-88-VELUX
www.veluxUSA.com

Page 187
© Andrea Rugg

Resource Guide (continued)

Garages

Page 194
Garage storage by
California Closets
1.888.336.9707
www.californiaclosets.com

Page 196-197
Garage cabinet design by
Don Mitchell/Mitchell Garage
Cabinet Systems
800-350-MGCS
www.MitchellGarageCabinetSystems.
com

For instructions on installing an attic
ladder, reference
*Black & Decker The Complete Guide
to a Clutter-free Home*
ISBN 978-1589234789 ©2009

Page 198
Garage by
Gladiator Garageworks/Whirlpool
Corporation
866-342-4089
www.gladiatorgw.com

Page 200
Garage storage by
GarageTek
866-664-2724
www.garagetek.com

Page 201
© Andrea Rugg

Page 202
Storage by
California Closets
1.888.336.9707
www.californiaclosets.com

Page 204 (top)
Hoist by
The Complete Garage Crossroads
Center
952-935-5200
www.thecompletegarage.com

Page 204 (bottom)
Hoist by
GarageTek
866-664-2724
www.garagetek.com

Page 205
Garage storage lift system by
Loft-it/Tivan, Inc.
952-440-8233
www.loft-it.com

Page 206-207
Garage storage by
Gladiator Garageworks/Whirlpool
Corporation
866-342-4089
www.gladiatorgw.com

Page 208
Athenée Mastrangelo
Professional Organizer, member NAPO
Action: Chaos
Serving Orlando and the Central
Florida Area
407-869-1683
www.actionchaos.com

Page 208
Garage design by
GarageTek
866-664-2724
www.garagetek.com

Page 209 (top)
Garage storage by
IKEA
800-434-4532
www.ikea.com

Page 209 (bottom)
Garage storage by
California Closets
1.888.336.9707
www.californiaclosets.com

Page 210
Garage storage by
Distinctions Cabinetry
800-203-0538
Distinctions Cabinetry is available
exclusively at Home Depot
www.distinctionscabinetry.com

Page 211 (top)
Garage storage by
Gladiator Garageworks/Whirlpool
Corporation
866-342-4089
www.gladiatorgw.com

Page 211 (bottom)
Storage by
California Closets
1.888.336.9707
www.californiaclosets.com

Page 212
Storage by
Rubbermaid
888-895-2110
www.rubbermaid.com

Page 213 (top)
Garage storage by
Stacks and Stacks
866-376-6856
www.stacksandstacks.com

Page 214
© Andrea Rugg

Page 215
Garage storage by
California Closets
1.888.336.9707
www.californiaclosets.com

Page s 216-217 (all)
© Sergio Piumatti

Page 218 (top)
Storage by
Rubbermaid
888-895-2110
www.rubbermaid.com

Page 218 (left)
Storage by
storeWALL™
414-224-0878
www.storewall.com

Page 219 (left)
Garage storage by
California Closets
1.888.336.9707
www.californiaclosets.com

Page 219 (right)
Garage storage by
Stacks and Stacks
866-376-6856
www.stacksandstacks.com

Page 220 (all)
Storage by
storeWALL™
414-224-0878
www.storewall.com

Page 222 –223 (both)
© Andrea Rugg

INDEX

INDEX